Textbook in History for Class XII

THEMES IN
INDIAN HISTORY
PART III

विद्या s मृतमश्नुते
NCERT

राष्ट्रीय शैक्षिक अनुसंधान और प्रशिक्षण परिषद्
NATIONAL COUNCIL OF EDUCATIONAL RESEARCH AND TRAINING

First Edition

July 2007   Sravana 1929

Reprinted

February 2008 Magha 1929
January 2009 Pausa 1930
January 2010 Magha 1931
November 2010 Kartika 1932
March 2013 Phalguna 1934
November 2013 Kartika 1935

PD 45T MJ

© *National Council of Educational Research and Training, 2007*

ISBN 81-7450-651-9 (Part I)
      81-7450-753-3 (Part II)
      81-7450-770-1 (Part III)

OFFICES OF THE PUBLICATION DIVISION, NCERT

NCERT Campus Sri Aurobindo Marg **New Delhi 110 016**	Phone : 011-26562708
108, 100 Feet Road Hosdakere Halli Extension Banashankari III Stage **Bangalore 560 085**	Phone : 080-26725740
Navjivan Trust Building P.O.Navjivan **Ahmedabad 380 014**	Phone : 079-27541446
CWC Campus Opp. Dhankal Bus Stop Panihati **Kolkata 700 114**	Phone : 033-25530454
CWC Complex Maligaon **Guwahati 781 021**	Phone : 0361-2674869

₹ 100.00

Printed on 80 GSM paper with NCERT watermark

Published at the Publication Division by the Secretary, National Council of Educational Research and Training, Sri Aurobindo Marg, New Delhi 110 016 and printed at Om Enterprises, D-75, Sector 63, Noida (UP)

Publication Team

Head, Publication Division	:	*Ashok Srivastava*
Chief Production Officer	:	*Kalyan Banerjee*
Chief Business Manager	:	*Gautam Ganguly*
Chief Editor (Contractual Service)	:	*Naresh Yadav*
Production Assistant	:	*Rajesh Pippal*

Cover and Layout
Art Creations, New Delhi

Cartography
Cartographic Design Agency

FOREWORD

The *National Curriculum Framework* (NCF), 2005, recommends that children's life at school must be linked to their life outside the school. This principle marks a departure from the legacy of bookish learning which continues to shape our system and causes a gap between the school, home and community. The syllabi and textbooks developed on the basis of NCF signify an attempt to implement this basic idea. They also attempt to discourage rote learning and the maintenance of sharp boundaries between different subject areas. We hope these measures will take us significantly further in the direction of a child-centred system of education outlined in the *National Policy on Education* (1986).

The success of this effort depends on the steps that school principals and teachers will take to encourage children to reflect on their own learning and to pursue imaginative activities and questions. We must recognise that, given space, time and freedom, children generate new knowledge by engaging with the information passed on to them by adults. Treating the prescribed textbook as the sole basis of examination is one of the key reasons why other resources and sites of learning are ignored. Inculcating creativity and initiative is possible if we perceive and treat children as participants in learning, not as receivers of a fixed body of knowledge.

These aims imply considerable change in school routines and mode of functioning. Flexibility in the daily time-table is as necessary as rigour in implementing the annual calendar so that the required number of teaching days are actually devoted to teaching. The methods used for teaching and evaluation will also determine how effective this textbook proves for making children's life at school a happy experience, rather than a source of stress or boredom. Syllabus designers have tried to address the problem of curricular burden by restructuring and reorienting knowledge at different stages with greater consideration for child psychology and the time available for teaching. The textbook attempts to enhance this endeavour by giving higher priority and space to opportunities for contemplation and wondering, discussion in small groups, and activities requiring hands-on experience.

The National Council of Educational Research and Training (NCERT) appreciates the hard work done by the textbook development committee responsible for this book. We wish to thank the Chairperson of the advisory group in Social Sciences, Professor Hari Vasudevan, and the Chief Advisor for this book,

Professor Neeladri Bhattacharya, Centre for Historical Studies, Jawaharlal Nehru University, New Delhi for guiding the work of this committee. Several teachers contributed to the development of this textbook; we are grateful to their principals for making this possible. We are indebted to the institutions and organisations which have generously permitted us to draw upon their resources, material and personnel. We are especially grateful to the members of the National Monitoring Committee, appointed by the Department of Secondary and Higher Education, Ministry of Human Resource Development under the Chairpersonship of Professor Mrinal Miri and Professor G.P. Deshpande, for their valuable time and contribution. As an organisation committed to systemic reform and continuous improvement in the quality of its products, NCERT welcomes comments and suggestions which will enable us to undertake further revision and refinement.

Director
New Delhi   National Council of Educational
20 November 2006   Research and Training

DEFINING THE FOCUS OF STUDY

What defines the focus of this book? What does it seek to do? How is it linked to what has been studied in earlier classes?

In Classes VI to VIII we looked at Indian history from early beginnings to modern times, with a focus on one chronological period in each year. Then in the books for Classes IX and X, the frame of reference changed. We looked at a shorter period of time, focusing specifically on a close study of the contemporary world. We moved beyond territorial boundaries, beyond the limits of nation states, to see how different people in different places have played their part in the making of the modern world. The history of India became connected to a wider inter-linked history. Subsequently in Class XI we studied *Themes in World History*, expanding our chronological focus, looking at the vast span of years from the beginning of human life to the present, but selecting only a set of themes for serious exploration. This year we will study *Themes in Indian History*.

The book begins with Harappa and ends with the framing of the Indian Constitution. What it offers is not a general survey of five millennia, but a close study of select themes. The history books in earlier years have already acquainted you with Indian history. It is time we explored some themes in greater detail.

In choosing the themes we have tried to ensure that we learn about developments in different spheres – economic, cultural, social, political, and religious – even as we attempt to break the boundaries between them. Some themes in the book will introduce you to the politics of the times and the nature of authority and power; others explore the way societies are organised, and the way they function and change; still others tell us about religious life and ritual practices, about the working of economies, and the changes within rural and urban societies.

Each of these themes will also allow you to have a closer look at the historians' craft. To retrieve the past, historians have to find sources that make the past accessible. But sources do not just reveal the past; historians have to grapple with sources, interpret them, and make them speak. This is what makes history exciting. The same sources can tell us new things if we ask new questions, and engage with them in new ways. So we need to see how historians read sources, and how they discover new things in old sources.

But historians do not only re-examine old records. They discover new ones. Sometimes these could be chance discoveries.

Archaeologists may unexpectedly come across seals and mounds that provide clues to the existence of a site of an ancient civilisation. Rummaging through the dusty records of a district collectorate a historian may trip over a bundle of records that contain legal cases of local disputes, and these may open up a new world of village life several centuries back. Yet are such discoveries only accidents? You may bump into a bundle of old records in an archive, open it up and see it, without discovering the significance of the source. The source may mean nothing to you unless you have relevant questions in mind. You have to track the source, read the text, follow the clues, and make the inter-connections before you can reconstruct the past. The physical discovery of a record does not simply open up the past. When Alexander Cunningham first saw a Harappan seal, he could make no sense of it. Only much later was the significance of the seals discovered.

In fact when historians begin to ask new questions, explore new themes, they have to often search for new types of sources. If we wish to know about revolutionaries and rebels, official sources can reveal only a partial picture, one that will be shaped by official censure and prejudice. We need to look for other sources – diaries of rebels, their personal letters, their writings and pronouncements. And these are not always easy to come by. If we have to understand experiences of people who suffered the trauma of partition, then oral sources might reveal more than written sources.

As the vision of history broadens, historians begin tracking new sources, searching for new clues to understand the past. And when that happens, the conception of what constitutes a source itself changes. There was a time when only written records were acknowledged as authentic. What was written could be verified, cited, and cross-checked. Oral evidence was never considered a valid source: who was to guarantee its authenticity and verifiability? This mistrust of oral sources has not yet disappeared, but oral evidence has been innovatively used to uncover experiences that no other record could reveal.

Through the book this year, you will enter the world of historians, accompany them in their search for new clues, and see how they carry on their dialogues with the past. You will witness the way they tease out meaning out of records, read inscriptions, excavate archaeological sites, make sense of beads and bones, interpret the epics, look at the stupas and buildings, examine paintings and photographs, interpret police reports and revenue records, and listen to the voices of the past. Each theme will explore the peculiarities and possibilities of one particular type of source. It will discuss what a source can tell and what it cannot.

This is the last part of *Themes in Indian History*.

NEELADRI BHATTACHARYA
Chief Advisor, History

TEXTBOOK DEVELOPMENT COMMITTEE

ACKNOWLEDGEMENTS

Themes in Indian History, Part III is the result of a collective effort of a large number of educationists, school teachers, historians, editors and designers. Each chapter was discussed and revised over months of intensive discussion. We thank all those who participated in the process.

Several people read the chapters and provided support. We thank in particular the members of the Monitoring Committee, Prof. J. S. Grewal and Shobha Bajpai for their useful comments on earlier drafts. Prof. Narayani Gupta, Prabhu Mohapatra and Tarun Saint offered valuable suggestions. Mahmood Farooqi suggested extracts for Chapter 11. Partha Shil, Akhila Yachuri and Sabyasachi Dasgupta gave research support.

Many institutions and individuals provided visual resources for the book: Victoria Memorial Museum and Library, Kolkata; Indira Gandhi National Centre for the Arts, New Delhi; Alkazi Foundation for the Arts, New Delhi; The Osian's Archive and Library Collection, Mumbai; CIVIC Archives, New Delhi; Photo Division, Government of India; South Asia Centre, University of Chicago. Chittaranjan Panda, Kaushik Bhowmik, Pratik Chakrabarty, and Rahab Alkazi took personal care in procuring visual material for illustrations. Juta and Jyotindra Jain opened up their vast collection of images with a generosity rare amongst collectors. We thank them all.

Shalini Advani and Shyama Warner did many rounds of editing with care and enthusiasm. Ritu Topa of Arrt Creations designed the book, working tirelessly to meet impossible deadlines. Albinus Tirkey provided technical support.

We have made every effort to acknowledge credits, but we apologise in advance for any omission that may have inadvertently taken place.

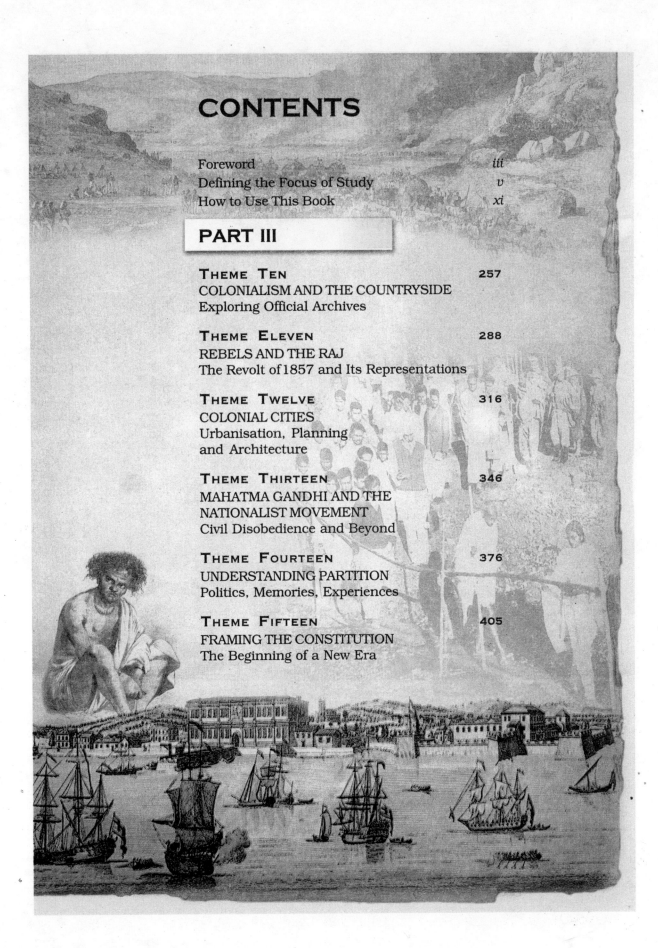

CONTENTS

HOW TO USE THIS BOOK

This is the last part of *Themes in Indian History.*

☑ Each chapter is divided into numbered sections and subsections to facilitate learning.

☑ You will also find other material enclosed in boxes.

These contain:

Short meanings	Additional information	More elaborate definitions

These are meant to assist and enrich the learning process, but are ***not intended for evaluation.***

☑ Each chapter ends with a set of ***timelines***. This is to be treated as background information, and ***not for evaluation***.

☑ There are ***figures, maps*** and ***sources*** numbered sequentially through each chapter.

    (a) **Figures** include illustrations of artefacts such as tools, pottery, seals, coins, ornaments etc. as well as of inscriptions, sculptures, paintings, buildings, archaeological sites, plans and photographs of people and places; visual material that historians use as sources.

    (b) Some chapters have **maps**.

Sources

    (c) **Sources** are enclosed within separate boxes: these contain excerpts from a wide variety of texts and inscriptions. Both visual and textual sources will help you acquire a feel for the clues that historians use. You will also see how historians analyse these clues. **The final examination can include excerpts from and/or illustrations of identical/similar material, providing you with an opportunity to handle these.**

☑ There are *two* categories of **intext questions:**

(a) those within a yellow box, which may be used for practice for **evaluation.**

(b) those with the caption ➲ Discuss... which are **not for evaluation**

☑ There are **four types** of assignments at the end of each chapter: These include:

 short questions

 short essays

 map work

projects

These are meant to provide practice for **the final assessment and evaluation.**

Hope you enjoy using this book.

COLONIALISM AND THE COUNTRYSIDE
EXPLORING OFFICIAL ARCHIVES

In this chapter you will see what colonial rule meant to those who lived in the countryside. You will meet the zamindars of Bengal, travel to the Rajmahal hills where the Paharias and the Santhals lived, and then move west to the Deccan. You will look at the way the English East India Company (E.I.C.) established its raj in the countryside, implemented its revenue policies, what these policies meant to different sections of people, and how they changed everyday lives.

Laws introduced by the state have consequences for people: they determine to an extent who grows richer and who poorer, who acquires new land and who loses the land they have lived on, where peasants go when they need money. As you will see, however, people were not only subject to the working of laws, they also resisted the law by acting according to what they believed to be just. In doing so people defined the way in which laws operated, thereby modifying their consequences.

You will also come to know about the sources that tell us about these histories, and the problems historians face in interpreting them. You will read about revenue records and surveys, journals and accounts left by surveyors and travellers, and reports produced by enquiry commissions.

Fig. 10.1
Cotton being carried from the village to the mandi,
Illustrated London News, *20 April 1861*

1. BENGAL AND THE ZAMINDARS

As you know, colonial rule was first established in Bengal. It is here that the earliest attempts were made to reorder rural society and establish a new regime of land rights and a new revenue system. Let us see what happened in Bengal in the early years of Company (E.I.C.) rule.

1.1 An auction in Burdwan

In 1797 there was an auction in Burdwan (present-day Bardhaman). It was a big public event. A number of *mahals* (estates) held by the Raja of Burdwan were being sold. The Permanent Settlement had come into operation in 1793. The East India Company had fixed the revenue that each zamindar had to pay. The estates of those who failed to pay were to be auctioned to recover the revenue. Since the raja had accumulated huge arrears, his estates had been put up for auction.

Numerous purchasers came to the auction and the estates were sold to the highest bidder. But the Collector soon discovered a strange twist to the tale. Many of the purchasers turned out to be servants and agents of the raja who had bought the lands on behalf of their master. Over 95 per cent of the sale at the auction was fictitious. The raja's estates had been publicly sold, but he remained in control of his zamindari.

Why had the raja failed to pay the revenue? Who were the purchasers at the auction? What does the story tell us about what was happening in the rural areas of eastern India at that time?

1.2 The problem of unpaid revenue

The estates of the Burdwan raj were not the only ones sold during the closing years of the eighteenth century. Over 75 per cent of the zamindaris changed hands after the Permanent Settlement.

In introducing the Permanent Settlement, British officials hoped to resolve the problems they had been facing since the conquest of Bengal. By the 1770s, the rural economy in Bengal was in crisis, with recurrent famines and declining agricultural output. Officials felt that agriculture, trade and the revenue resources of the state could all be developed by encouraging investment in agriculture. This could be done by securing rights of property and permanently fixing the rates of

Raja (literally king) was a term that was often used to designate powerful zamindars.

Fig. 10.2
Burdwan raja's City Palace on Diamond Harbour Road, Calcutta
By the late nineteenth century many rich zamindars of Bengal had city palaces with ballrooms, large grounds, entrance porches supported by Corinthian columns like these.

revenue demand. If the revenue demand of the state was permanently fixed, then the Company could look forward to a regular flow of revenue, while entrepreneurs could feel sure of earning a profit from their investment, since the state would not siphon it off by increasing its claim. The process, officials hoped, would lead to the emergence of a class of yeomen farmers and rich landowners who would have the capital and enterprise to improve agriculture. Nurtured by the British, this class would also be loyal to the Company.

The problem, however, lay in identifying individuals who could both improve agriculture and contract to pay the fixed revenue to the state. After a prolonged debate amongst Company officials, the Permanent Settlement was made with the rajas and *taluqdars* of Bengal. They were now classified as zamindars, and they had to pay the revenue demand that was fixed in perpetuity. In terms of this definition, the zamindar was not a landowner in the village, but a revenue Collector of the state.

Zamindars had several (sometimes as many as 400) villages under them. In Company calculations the villages within one zamindari formed one revenue estate. The Company fixed the total demand over the entire estate whose revenue the zamindar contracted to pay. The zamindar collected rent from the different villages, paid the revenue to the Company, and retained the difference as his income. He was expected to pay the Company regularly, failing which his estate could be auctioned.

1.3 Why zamindars defaulted on payments

Company officials felt that a fixed revenue demand would give zamindars a sense of security and, assured of returns on their investment, encourage them to improve their estates. In the early decades after the Permanent Settlement, however, zamindars regularly failed to pay the revenue demand and unpaid balances accumulated.

The reasons for this failure were various. First: the initial demands were very high. This was because it was felt that if the demand was fixed for all time to come, the Company would never be able to claim a share of increased income from land when prices rose and cultivation expanded. To minimise this anticipated loss, the Company pegged the revenue

Fig. 10.3
Charles Cornwallis (1738-1805), painted by Thomas Gainsborough, 1785
He was the commander of the British forces during the American War of Independence and the Governor General of Bengal when the Permanent Settlement was introduced there in 1793.

Taluqdar literally means "one who holds a *taluq*" or a connection. *Taluq* came to refer to a territorial unit.

demand high, arguing that the burden on zamindars would gradually decline as agricultural production expanded and prices rose.

Second: this high demand was imposed in the 1790s, a time when the prices of agricultural produce were depressed, making it difficult for the *ryots* to pay their dues to the zamindar. If the zamindar could not collect the rent, how could he pay the Company? Third: the revenue was invariable, regardless of the harvest, and had to be paid punctually. In fact, according to the Sunset Law, if payment did not come in by sunset of the specified date, the zamindari was liable to be auctioned. Fourth: the Permanent Settlement initially limited the power of the zamindar to collect rent from the *ryot* and manage his zamindari.

The Company had recognised the zamindars as important, but it wanted to control and regulate them, subdue their authority and restrict their autonomy. The zamindars' troops were disbanded, customs duties abolished, and their "*cutcheries*" (courts) brought under the supervision of a Collector appointed by the Company. Zamindars lost their power to organise local justice and the local police. Over time the collectorate emerged as an alternative centre of authority, severely restricting what the zamindar could do. In one case, when a raja failed to pay the revenue, a Company official was speedily dispatched to his zamindari with explicit instructions "to take charge of the District and to use the most effectual means to destroy all the influence and the authority of the raja and his officers".

At the time of rent collection, an officer of the zamindar, usually the *amlah*, came around to the village. But rent collection was a perennial problem. Sometimes bad harvests and low prices made payment of dues difficult for the *ryots*. At other times *ryots* deliberately delayed payment. Rich *ryots* and village headmen – *jotedars* and *mandals* – were only too happy to see the zamindar in trouble. The zamindar could therefore not easily assert his power over them. Zamindars could prosecute defaulters, but the judicial process was long drawn. In Burdwan alone there were over 30,000 pending suits for arrears of rent payment in 1798.

> *Ryot* is the way the term *raiyat*, used to designate peasants (Chapter 8), was spelt in British records. *Ryots* in Bengal did not always cultivate the land directly, but leased it out to under-*ryots*.

1.4 The rise of the *jotedars*

While many zamindars were facing a crisis at the end of the eighteenth century, a group of rich peasants were consolidating their position in the villages. In Francis Buchanan's survey of the Dinajpur district in North Bengal we have a vivid description of this class of rich peasants known as *jotedars*. By the early nineteenth century, *jotedars* had acquired vast areas of land – sometimes as much as several thousand acres. They controlled local trade as well as moneylending, exercising immense power over the poorer cultivators of the region. A large part of their land was cultivated through sharecroppers (*adhiyars* or *bargadars*) who brought their own ploughs, laboured in the field, and handed over half the produce to the *jotedars* after the harvest.

Within the villages, the power of *jotedars* was more effective than that of zamindars. Unlike zamindars who often lived in urban areas, *jotedars* were located in the villages and exercised direct control over a considerable section of poor villagers. They fiercely resisted efforts by zamindars to increase the *jama* of the village, prevented zamindari officials from executing their duties, mobilised *ryots* who were dependent on them, and deliberately delayed payments of revenue to the zamindar. In fact, when the estates of the zamindars were auctioned for failure to make revenue payment, *jotedars* were often amongst the purchasers.

The *jotedars* were most powerful in North Bengal, although rich peasants and village headmen were emerging as commanding figures in the countryside in other parts of Bengal as well. In some places they were called *haoladars*, elsewhere they were known as *gantidars* or *mandals*. Their rise inevitably weakened zamindari authority.

Fig. 10.4
Bengal village scene, painted by George Chinnery, 1820
Chinnery stayed in India for 23 years (1802-25), painting portraits, landscapes and scenes of the everyday life of the common people. *Jotedars* and moneylenders in rural Bengal lived in houses like the one you see on the right.

Source 1

The *jotedars* of Dinajpur

Buchanan described the ways in which the *jotedars* of Dinajpur in North Bengal resisted being disciplined by the zamindar and undermined his power:

Landlords do not like this class of men, but it is evident that they are absolutely necessary, unless the landlords themselves would advance money to their necessitous tenantry ...

The *jotedars* who cultivate large portions of lands are very refractory, and know that the zamindars have no power over them. They pay only a few rupees on account of their revenue and then fall in balance almost every *kist* (instalment), they hold more lands than they are entitled to by their *pottahs* (deeds of contract). Should the zamindar's officers, in consequence, summon them to the *cutcherry*, and detain them for one or two hours with a view to reprimand them, they immediately go and complain at the Fouzdarry Thanna (police station) for imprisonment and at the munsiff's (a judicial officer at the lower court) *cutcherry* for being dishonoured and whilst the causes continue unsettled, they instigate the petty *ryots* not to pay their revenue consequently ...

> ⊃ Describe the ways in which the *jotedars* resisted the authority of the zamindars.

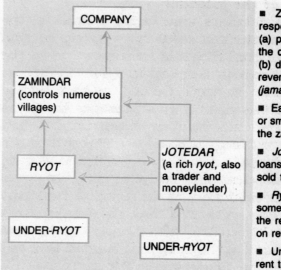

Fig.10.5
Power in rural Bengal

- Zamindars were responsible for:
  (a) paying revenue to the company
  (b) distributing the revenue demand *(jama)* over villages.

- Each village *ryot*, big or small, paid rent to the zamindar.

- *Jotedars* gave out loans to other *ryots* and sold their produce.

- *Ryots* cultivated some land and gave out the rest to under-*ryots* on rent.

- Under-*ryots* paid rent to the *ryots*.

> ⊃ Read the text accompanying Fig.10.5 carefully and insert the following terms in appropriate places along the arrows: rent, revenue, interest, loan, produce

1.5 The zamindars resist

The authority of the zamindars in rural areas, however, did not collapse. Faced with an exorbitantly high revenue demand and possible auction of their estates, they devised ways of surviving the pressures. New contexts produced new strategies.

Fictitious sale was one such strategy. It involved a series of manoeuvres. The Raja of Burdwan, for instance, first transferred some of his zamindari to his mother, since the Company had decreed that the property of women would not be taken over. Then, as a second move, his agents manipulated the auctions. The revenue demand of the Company was deliberately withheld, and unpaid balances were allowed to accumulate. When a part of the estate was auctioned, the zamindar's men bought the property, outbidding other purchasers. Subsequently they refused to pay up the purchase money, so that the estate had to be resold. Once again it was bought by the zamindar's agents, once again the purchase money was not paid, and once again there was an auction. This process was repeated endlessly, exhausting the state, and the other bidders at the auction. At last the estate was sold at a low price back to the zamindar. The zamindar never paid the full revenue demand; the Company rarely recovered the unpaid balances that had piled up.

Such transactions happened on a grand scale. Between 1793 and 1801 four big zamindaris of Bengal, including Burdwan, made *benami* purchases that collectively yielded as much as Rs 30 lakh. Of the total sales at the auctions, over 15 per cent were fictitious.

There were other ways in which zamindars circumvented displacement. When people from outside the zamindari bought an estate at an auction, they could not always take possession. At times their agents would be attacked by *lathyals* of the former zamindar. Sometimes even the *ryots* resisted the entry of outsiders. They felt bound to their own zamindar through a sense of loyalty and perceived him as a figure of authority and themselves as his *proja* (subjects). The sale of the zamindari disturbed their sense of identity, their pride. The zamindars therefore were not easily displaced.

By the beginning of the nineteenth century the depression in prices was over. Thus those who had survived the troubles of the 1790s consolidated their power. Rules of revenue payment were also made somewhat flexible. As a result, the zamindar's power over the villages was strengthened. It was only during the Great Depression of the 1930s that they finally collapsed and the *jotedars* consolidated their power in the countryside.

Fig. 10.6
Maharaja Mehtab Chand (1820-79)
When the Permanent Settlement was imposed, Tejchand was the Raja of Burdwan. Subsequently under Mehtab Chand the estate prospered. Mehtab Chand helped the British during the Santhal rebellion and the 1857 revolt.

1.6 The Fifth Report

Many of the changes we are discussing were documented in detail in a report that was submitted to the British Parliament in 1813. It was the fifth of a series of reports on the administration and activities of the East India Company in India. Often referred to as the Fifth Report, it ran into 1002 pages, of which over 800 pages were appendices that reproduced petitions of zamindars and *ryots*, reports of collectors from different districts, statistical tables on revenue returns, and notes on the revenue and judicial administration of Bengal and Madras (present-day Tamil Nadu) written by officials.

From the time the Company established its rule in Bengal in the mid-1760s, its activities were closely watched and debated in England. There were many

Benami, literally anonymous, is a term used in Hindi and several other Indian languages for transactions made in the name of a fictitious or relatively insignificant person, whereas the real beneficiary remains unnamed.

Lathyal, literally one who wields the *lathi* or stick, functioned as a strongman of the zamindar.

groups in Britain who were opposed to the monopoly that the East India Company had over trade with India and China. These groups wanted a revocation of the Royal Charter that gave the Company this monopoly. An increasing number of private traders wanted a share in the India trade, and the industrialists of Britain were keen to open up the Indian market for British manufactures. Many political groups argued that the conquest of Bengal was benefiting only the East India Company but not the British nation as a whole. Information about Company misrule and maladministration was hotly debated in Britain and incidents of the greed and corruption of Company officials were widely publicised in the press. The British Parliament passed a series of Acts in the late eighteenth century to regulate and control Company rule in India. It forced the Company to produce regular reports on the administration of India and appointed committees to enquire into the affairs of the Company. The Fifth Report was one such report produced by a Select Committee. It became the basis of intense parliamentary debates on the nature of the East India Company's rule in India.

Fig. 10.7
Andul Raj Palace
The ruins of palaces are a visible sign of the end of an era. Satyajit Ray's famous film *Jalshaghar*, on the decline of the aristocratic zamindari style of living, was shot in Andul Raj Palace.

For over a century and a half, the Fifth Report has shaped our conception of what happened in rural Bengal in the late eighteenth century. The evidence contained in the Fifth Report is invaluable. But official reports like this have to be read carefully. We need to know who wrote the reports and why they were written. In fact, recent researches show that the arguments and evidence offered by the Fifth Report cannot be accepted uncritically.

Researchers have carefully examined the archives of various Bengal zamindars and the local records of the districts to write about the history of colonial rule in rural Bengal. They indicate that, intent on criticising the maladministration of the company, the Fifth Report exaggerated the collapse of traditional zamindari power, as also overestimated the scale on which zamindars were losing their land. As we have seen, even when zamindaris were auctioned, zamindars were not always displaced, given the ingenious methods they used to retain their zamindaris.

Source 2

From the Fifth Report

Referring to the condition of zamindars and the auction of lands, the Fifth Report stated:

> The revenue was not realised with punctuality, and lands to a considerable extent were periodically exposed to sale by auction. In the native year 1203, corresponding with 1796-97, the land advertised for sale comprehended a *jumma* or assessment of *sicca* rupees 28,70,061, the extent of land actually sold bore a *jumma* or assessment of 14,18,756, and the amount of purchase money *sicca* rupees 17,90,416. In 1204, corresponding with 1797-98, the land advertised was for *sicca* rupees 26,66,191, the quantity sold was for *sicca* rupees 22,74,076, and the purchase money *sicca* rupees 21,47,580. Among the defaulters were some of the oldest families of the country. Such were the rajahs of Nuddea, Rajeshaye, Bishenpore (all districts of Bengal), ... and others, the dismemberment of whose estates at the end of each succeeding year, threatened them with poverty and ruin, and in some instances presented difficulties to the revenue officers, in their efforts to preserve undiminished the amount of public assessment.

➲ From the tone in which evidence is recorded, what do you think is the attitude of the report to the facts narrated? What is the Report trying to say through the figures? Can you think of any problem in making long-term generalisations from these figures of two years?

➲ Discuss...
Compare the account of the zamindars you have just read with that in Chapter 8.

2. THE HOE AND THE PLOUGH

Let us now shift our focus from the wetlands of Bengal to drier zones, from a region of settled cultivation to one where shifting agriculture was practised. You will see the changes that came about when the frontiers of the peasant economy expanded outwards, swallowing up pastures and forests in the Rajmahal hills. You will also see how these changes created a variety of conflicts within the region.

2.1 In the hills of Rajmahal

In the early nineteenth century, Buchanan travelled through the Rajmahal hills. From his description, the hills appeared impenetrable, a zone where few travellers ventured, an area that signified danger. Wherever he went, people were hostile, apprehensive of officials and unwilling to talk to them. In many instances they deserted their villages and absconded.

Who were these hill folk? Why were they so apprehensive of Buchanan's visit? Buchanan's journal gives us tantalising glimpses of these hill folk in the early nineteenth century. His journal was written as a diary of places he visited, people he encountered, and practices he saw. It raises questions in our mind, but does not always help us answer them. It tells us about a moment in time, but not about the longer history of people and places. For that historians have to turn to other records.

If we look at late-eighteenth-century revenue records, we learn that these hill folk were known as Paharias. They lived around the Rajmahal hills, subsisting on forest produce and practising shifting cultivation. They cleared patches of forest by cutting bushes and burning the undergrowth. On these patches, enriched by the potash from the ash, the Paharias grew a variety of pulses and millets for consumption. They scratched the ground lightly with hoes, cultivated the cleared land for a few years, then left it fallow so that it could recover its fertility, and moved to a new area.

From the forests they collected *mahua* (a flower) for food, silk cocoons and resin for sale, and wood for charcoal production. The undergrowth that spread like a mat below the trees and the patches of grass that covered the lands left fallow provided pasture for cattle.

Who was Buchanan?

Francis Buchanan was a physician who came to India and served in the Bengal Medical Service (from 1794 to 1815). For a few years he was surgeon to the Governor-General of India, Lord Wellesley. During his stay in Calcutta (present-day Kolkata), he organised a zoo that became the Calcutta Alipore Zoo; he was also in charge of the Botanical Gardens for a short period. On the request of the Government of Bengal, he undertook detailed surveys of the areas under the jurisdiction of the British East India Company. In 1815 he fell ill and returned to England. Upon his mother's death, he inherited her property and assumed her family name Hamilton. So he is often called Buchanan-Hamilton.

Fig. 10.8
A view of a hill village in Rajmahal, painted by William Hodges, 1782
William Hodges was a British artist who accompanied Captain Cook on his second voyage
to the Pacific (1772-75), and then came to India. In 1781 he became a friend of Augustus
Cleveland, the Collector of Bhagalpur. On the invitation of Cleveland, Hodges accompanied
him to the Jangal Mahals in 1782, and painted a set of aquatints. Like many other
British painters of the time, Hodges searched for the picturesque. Artists in search of the
picturesque were inspired by the ideals of Romanticism, a tradition of thought that
celebrated nature and admired its magnificence and power. Romantics felt that to commune
with nature the artist had to represent nature as an idyll, uncorrupted by modern
civilisation, discover unknown landscapes, and appreciate the sublime play of light and
shade. It is in search of this unknown that Hodges went to the Rajmahal hills. He found
flat landscapes monotonous, and discovered beauty in roughness, irregularity and variety.
A landscape that colonial officials found dangerous and wild, peopled by turbulent tribes,
appears in the paintings of Hodges as exotic and idyllic.

⊃ Look at the painting and identify the ways in which it represents the
traditions of the picturesque.

The life of the Paharias – as hunters, shifting
cultivators, food gatherers, charcoal producers,
silkworm rearers – was thus intimately connected to
the forest. They lived in hutments within tamarind
groves, and rested in the shade of mango trees. They
considered the entire region as their land, the basis

Aquatint is a picture produced
by cutting into a copper sheet
with acid and then printing it.

Fig. 10.9
A view of Jangal territory,
painted by William Hodges
Here you can see the forested
low hills and the rocky upper
ranges, nowhere actually above
2,000 feet. By centring the hills
and viewing them from below,
Hodges emphasises their
inaccessibility.

➲ Look at Figs. 10.8 and
10.9. Describe how the
pictures represent the
relationship between tribal
people and nature.

of their identity as well as survival; and they resisted
the intrusion of outsiders. Their chiefs maintained
the unity of the group, settled disputes, and led the
tribe in battles with other tribes and plainspeople.

With their base in the hills, the Paharias regularly
raided the plains where settled agriculturists lived.
These raids were necessary for survival, particularly
in years of scarcity; they were a way of asserting
power over settled communities; and they were a
means of negotiating political relations with
outsiders. The zamindars on the plains had to often
purchase peace by paying a regular tribute to the
hill chiefs. Traders similarly gave a small amount
to the hill folk for permission to use the passes
controlled by them. Once the toll was paid, the
Paharia chiefs protected the traders, ensuring that
their goods were not plundered by anyone.

This negotiated peace was somewhat fragile. It
broke down in the last decades of the eighteenth
century when the frontiers of settled agriculture were
being aggressively extended in eastern India. The
British encouraged forest clearance, and zamindars
and *jotedars* turned uncultivated lands into rice
fields. To the British, extension of settled agriculture
was necessary to enlarge the sources of land
revenue, produce crops for export, and establish
the basis of a settled, ordered society. They also
associated forests with wildness, and saw forest
people as savage, unruly, primitive, and difficult to
govern. So they felt that forests had to be cleared,

settled agriculture established, and forest people tamed, civilised and persuaded to give up hunting and take to plough agriculture.

As settled agriculture expanded, the area under forests and pastures contracted. This sharpened the conflict between hill folk and settled cultivators. The former began to raid settled villages with increasing regularity, carrying away food grains and cattle. Exasperated colonial officials tried desperately to control and subdue the Paharias. But they found the task difficult.

In the 1770s the British embarked on a brutal policy of extermination, hunting the Paharias down and killing them. Then, by the 1780s, Augustus Cleveland, the Collector of Bhagalpur, proposed a policy of pacification. Paharia chiefs were given an annual allowance and made responsible for the proper conduct of their men. They were expected to maintain order in their localities and discipline their own people. Many Paharia chiefs refused the allowances. Those who accepted, most often lost authority within the community. Being in the pay of the colonial government, they came to be perceived as subordinate employees or stipendiary chiefs.

As the pacification campaigns continued, the Paharias withdrew deep into the mountains, insulating themselves from hostile forces, and carrying on a war with outsiders. So when Buchanan travelled through the region in the winter of 1810-11 the Paharias naturally viewed him with suspicion and distrust. The experience of pacification campaigns and memories of brutal repression shaped their perception of British infiltration into the area. Every white man appeared to represent a power that was destroying their way of life and means of survival, snatching away their control over their forests and lands.

By this time in fact there were newer intimations of danger. Santhals were pouring into the area, clearing forests, cutting down timber, ploughing land and growing rice and cotton. As the lower hills were taken over by Santhal settlers, the Paharias receded deeper into the Rajmahal hills. If Paharia life was symbolised by the hoe, which they used for shifting cultivation, the settlers came to represent the power of the plough. The battle between the hoe and the plough was a long one.

2.2 The Santhals: Pioneer settlers

At the end of 1810, Buchanan crossed Ganjuria Pahar, which was part of the Rajmahal ranges, passed through the rocky country beyond, and reached a village. It was an old village but the land around had been recently cleared to extend cultivation. Looking at the landscape, Buchanan found evidence of the region having been transformed through "proper application of human labour". He wrote: "Gunjuriya is just sufficiently cultivated to show what a glorious country this might be made. I think its beauty and riches might be made equal to almost any in the universe." The soil here was rocky but "uncommonly fine", and nowhere had Buchanan seen finer tobacco and mustard. On enquiry he discovered that the frontiers of cultivation here had been extended by the Santhals. They had moved into this area around 1800, displaced the hill folk who lived on these lower slopes, cleared the forests and settled the land.

How did the Santhals reach the Rajmahal hills? The Santhals had begun to come into Bengal around the 1780s. Zamindars hired them to reclaim land and expand cultivation, and British officials invited them to settle in the Jangal Mahals. Having failed to subdue the Paharias and transform them into settled agriculturists, the British turned to the Santhals. The Paharias refused to cut forests, resisted touching the plough, and continued to be

Fig. 10.10
Hill village in Santhal country,
Illustrated London News,
23 February 1856
This village in the lower Rajmahal hills was sketched by Walter Sherwill in the early 1850s.
The village appears to be peaceful, calm and idyllic. Life seems unaffected by the outside world.

⊃ Contrast this image of the Santhal village with Fig. 10.12.

turbulent. The Santhals, by contrast, appeared to be ideal settlers, clearing forests and ploughing the land with vigour.

The Santhals were given land and persuaded to settle in the foothills of Rajmahal. By 1832 a large area of land was demarcated as Damin-i-Koh. This was declared to be the land of the Santhals. They were to live within it, practise plough agriculture, and become settled peasants. The land grant to the Santhals stipulated that at least one-tenth of the area was to be cleared and cultivated within the first ten years. The territory was surveyed and mapped. Enclosed with boundary pillars, it was separated from both the world of the settled agriculturists of the plains and the Paharias of the hills.

After the demarcation of Damin-i-Koh, Santhal settlements expanded rapidly. From 40 Santhal villages in the area in 1838, as many as 1,473 villages had come up by 1851. Over the same period, the Santhal population increased from a mere 3,000 to over 82,000. As cultivation expanded, an increased volume of revenue flowed into the Company's coffers.

Santhal myths and songs of the nineteenth century refer very frequently to a long history of travel: they represent the Santhal past as one of continuous mobility, a tireless search for a place to settle. Here in the Damin-i-Koh their journey seemed to have come to an end.

When the Santhals settled on the peripheries of the Rajmahal hills, the Paharias resisted but were ultimately forced to withdraw deeper into the hills. Restricted from moving down to the lower hills and valleys, they were confined to the dry interior and to the more barren and rocky upper hills. This severely affected their lives, impoverishing them in the long term. Shifting agriculture depended on the ability to move to newer and newer land and utilisation of the natural fertility of the soil. When the most fertile soils became inaccessible to them, being part of the Damin, the Paharias could not effectively sustain their mode of cultivation. When the forests of the region were cleared for cultivation the hunters amongst them also faced problems. The Santhals, by contrast, gave up their earlier life of mobility and settled down, cultivating a range of commercial crops for the market, and dealing with traders and moneylenders.

Fig. 10.11
Sidhu Manjhi, the leader of the Santhal rebellion

The Santhals, however, soon found that the land they had brought under cultivation was slipping away from their hands. The state was levying heavy taxes on the land that the Santhals had cleared, moneylenders (*dikus*) were charging them high rates of interest and taking over the land when debts remained unpaid, and zamindars were asserting control over the Damin area.

By the 1850s, the Santhals felt that the time had come to rebel against zamindars, moneylenders and the colonial state, in order to create an ideal world for themselves where they would rule. It was after the Santhal Revolt (1855-56) that the Santhal Pargana was created, carving out 5,500 square miles from the districts of Bhagalpur and Birbhum. The colonial state hoped that by creating a new territory for the Santhals and imposing some special laws within it, the Santhals could be conciliated.

Fig. 10.12
Santhals fight the sepoys of the British Raj, Illustrated London News, *23 February 1856*
The rebellion changed the British perception of the Santhals. Villages that had earlier seemed calm and peaceful (Fig. 10.10) now appeared to have become places of violent and savage deeds.

➲ Imagine you are a reader of the *Illustrated London News* in England. How will you react to the images depicted in Figs. 10.12, 10.13 and 10.14? What image of the Santhals would these pictures create in your mind?

Fig. 10.13
Burning of Santhal villages, Illustrated London News, *23 February 1856*
After the rebellion was crushed, the region was searched, suspects were picked up, and villages set on fire. Images of the burning villages were shown to the public in England – once again as a demonstration of the might of the British and their ability to crush rebellion and impose colonial order.

Fig. 10.14
Santhal prisoners being taken away, Illustrated London News, *1856*
Notice how images like this one seek to convey political messages. At the centre you can see British officials triumphantly riding on an elephant. One officer on a horse is smoking a hookah: a picture that emphasises that the time of trouble was over, the rebellion had been crushed. The rebels are now in chains, being taken away to jail escorted and surrounded by soldiers of the Company.

Source 3

Buchanan on the Santhals

Buchanan wrote:

They are very clever in clearing new lands, but live meanly. Their huts have no fence, and the walls are made of small sticks placed upright, close together and plastered within with clay. They are small and slovenly, and too flat-roofed, with very little arch.

Source 4

The rocks near Kaduya

Buchanan's journal is packed with observations like the following:

About a mile farther on, (I) came to a low ledge of rocks without any evident strata; it is a small grained granite with reddish feldspar, with quartz and black mica ... More than half a mile from thence, I came to another rock not stratified, and consisting of very fine-grained granite with yellowish feldspar, whitish quartz and black mica.

2.3 The accounts of Buchanan

We have been drawing on Buchanan's account, but while reading his reports we should not forget that he was an employee of the British East India Company. His journeys were not simply inspired by the love of landscape and the desire to discover the unknown. He marched everywhere with a large army of people – draughtsmen, surveyors, palanquin bearers, coolies. The costs of the travels were borne by the East India Company since it needed the information that Buchanan was expected to collect. Buchanan had specific instructions about what he had to look for and what he had to record. When he arrived at a village with his army of people, he was immediately perceived as an agent of the *sarkar*.

As the Company consolidated its power and expanded its commerce, it looked for natural resources it could control and exploit. It surveyed landscapes and revenue sources, organised voyages of discovery, and sent its geologists and geographers, its botanists and medical men to collect information. Buchanan, undoubtedly an extraordinary observer, was one such individual. Everywhere Buchanan went, he obsessively observed the stones and rocks and the different strata and layers of soil. He searched for minerals and stones that were commercially valuable, he recorded all signs of iron ore and mica, granite and saltpetre. He carefully observed local practices of salt-making and iron-ore-mining.

When Buchanan wrote about a landscape, he most often described not just what he saw, what the landscape was like, but also how it could be transformed and made more productive – what crops could be cultivated, which trees cut down, and which ones grown. And we must remember that his vision and his priorities were different from those of the local inhabitants: his assessment of what was necessary was shaped by the commercial concerns of the Company and modern Western notions of what constituted progress. He was inevitably critical of the lifestyles of forest dwellers and felt that forests had to be turned into agricultural lands.

Source 5

On clearance and settled cultivation

Passing through one village in the lower Rajmahal hills, Buchanan wrote:

> The view of the country is exceedingly fine, the cultivation, especially the narrow valleys of rice winding in all directions, the cleared lands with scattered trees, and the rocky hills are in perfection; all that is wanted is some appearance of progress in the area and a vastly extended and improved cultivation, of which the country is highly susceptible. Plantations of Asan and Palas, for Tessar (Tassar silk worms) and Lac, should occupy the place of woods to as great an extent as the demand will admit; the remainder might be all cleared, and the greater part cultivated, while what is not fit for the purpose, might rear Plamira (palmyra) and Mowa (*mahua*).

⊃ Discuss...

What does Buchanan's description tell us about his ideas of development? Illustrate your argument by quoting from the excerpts. If you were a Paharia forest dweller how would you have reacted to these ideas?

3. A REVOLT IN THE COUNTRYSIDE
THE BOMBAY DECCAN

You have read about how the lives of peasants and zamindars of colonial Bengal and the Paharias and Santhals of the Rajmahal hills were changing. Now let us move across to western India, and to a later period, and explore what was happening in the countryside in the Bombay Deccan.

One way of exploring such changes is by focusing on a peasant revolt. In such climactic times rebels express their anger and fury; they rise against what they perceive to be injustice and the causes of their suffering. If we try to understand the premises of their resentment, and peel the layers of their anger, we get a glimpse of their life and experience that is otherwise hidden from us. Revolts also produce records that historians can look at. Alarmed by the actions of rebels and keen on restoring order, state authorities do not simply repress a rebellion. They try and understand it, enquire into its causes so that policies can be formulated and peace established. These enquiries produce evidence that historians can explore.

Through the nineteenth century, peasants in various parts of India rose in revolt against

Source 6

On that day in Supa

On 16 May 1875, the District Magistrate of Poona wrote to the Police Commissioner:

On arrival at Supa on Saturday 15 May I learnt of the disturbance.

One house of a moneylender was burnt down; about a dozen were forcibly broken into and completely gutted of their content. Account papers, bonds, grains, country cloth were burnt in the street where heaps of ashes are still to be seen.

The chief constable apprehended 50 persons. Stolen property worth Rs 2000 was recovered. The estimated loss is over Rs 25,000. Moneylenders claim it is over 1 lakh.

DECCAN RIOTS COMMISSION

A *sahukar* was someone who acted as both a moneylender and a trader.

⊃ The words and terms used by a writer often tell us something about his or her prejudices. Read Source 7 carefully and pick out the terms that indicate any prejudices of the writer. Discuss how a *ryot* of the area would have described the same situation.

moneylenders and grain dealers. One such revolt occurred in 1875 in the Deccan.

3.1 Account books are burnt

The movement began at Supa, a large village in Poona (present-day Pune) district. It was a market centre where many shopkeepers and moneylenders lived. On 12 May 1875, *ryots* from surrounding rural areas gathered and attacked the shopkeepers, demanding their *bahi khatas* (account books) and debt bonds. They burnt the *khatas*, looted grain shops, and in some cases set fire to the houses of *sahukars*.

From Poona the revolt spread to Ahmednagar. Then over the next two months it spread even further, over an area of 6,500 square km. More than thirty villages were affected. Everywhere the pattern was the same: *sahukars* were attacked, account books burnt and debt bonds destroyed. Terrified of peasant attacks, the *sahukars* fled the villages, very often leaving their property and belongings behind.

As the revolt spread, British officials saw the spectre of 1857 (see Chapter 11). Police posts were established in villages to frighten rebellious peasants into submission. Troops were quickly called in; 951 people were arrested, and many convicted. But it took several months to bring the countryside under control.

Source 7

A newspaper report

The following report, titled 'The ryot and the moneylender', appeared in the *Native Opinion* (6 June 1876), and was quoted in *Report of the Native Newspapers of Bombay:*

They (the *ryots*) first place spies on the boundaries of their villages to see if any Government officers come, and to give timely intimation of their arrival to the offenders. They then assemble in a body and go to the houses of their creditors, and demand from them a surrender of their bonds and other documents, and threaten them in case of refusal with assault and plunder. If any Government officer happens to approach the villages where the above is taking place, the spies give intimation to the offenders and the latter disperse in time.

Why the burning of bonds and deeds? Why this revolt? What does it tell us about the Deccan countryside and about agrarian changes under colonial rule? Let us look at this longer history of changes over the nineteenth century.

3.2 A new revenue system

As British rule expanded from Bengal to other parts of India, new systems of revenue were imposed. The Permanent Settlement was rarely extended to any region beyond Bengal.

Why was this so? One reason was that after 1810, agricultural prices rose, increasing the value of harvest produce, and enlarging the income of the Bengal zamindars. Since the revenue demand was fixed under the Permanent Settlement, the colonial state could not claim any share of this enhanced income. Keen on expanding its financial resources, the colonial government had to think of ways to maximise its land revenue. So in territories annexed in the nineteenth century, temporary revenue settlements were made.

There were other reasons too. When officials devise policies, their thinking is deeply shaped by economic theories they are familiar with. By the 1820s, the economist David Ricardo was a celebrated figure in England. Colonial officials had learnt Ricardian ideas during their college years. In Maharashtra when British officials set about formulating the terms of the early settlement in the 1820s, they operated with some of these ideas.

According to Ricardian ideas, a landowner should have a claim only to the "average rent" that prevailed at a given time. When the land yielded more than this "average rent", the landowner had a surplus that the state needed to tax. If tax was not levied, cultivators were likely to turn into rentiers, and their surplus income was unlikely to be productively invested in the improvement of the land. Many British officials in India thought that the history of Bengal confirmed Ricardo's theory. There the zamindars seemed to have turned into rentiers, leasing out land and living on the rental incomes. It was therefore necessary, the British officials now felt, to have a different system.

The revenue system that was introduced in the Bombay Deccan came to be known as the *ryotwari*

Rentier is a term used to designate people who live on rental income from property.

settlement. Unlike the Bengal system, the revenue was directly settled with the *ryot*. The average income from different types of soil was estimated, the revenue-paying capacity of the *ryot* was assessed and a proportion of it fixed as the share of the state. The lands were resurveyed every 30 years and the revenue rates increased. Therefore the revenue demand was no longer permanent.

3.3 Revenue demand and peasant debt

The first revenue settlement in the Bombay Deccan was made in the 1820s. The revenue that was demanded was so high that in many places peasants deserted their villages and migrated to new regions. In areas of poor soil and fluctuating rainfall the problem was particularly acute. When rains failed and harvests were poor, peasants found it impossible to pay the revenue. However, the collectors in charge of revenue collection were keen on demonstrating their efficiency and pleasing their superiors. So they went about extracting payment with utmost severity. When someone failed to pay, his crops were seized and a fine was imposed on the whole village.

By the 1830s the problem became more severe. Prices of agricultural products fell sharply after 1832 and did not recover for over a decade and a half. This meant a further decline in peasants' income. At the same time the countryside was devastated by a famine that struck in the years 1832-34. One-third of the cattle of the Deccan were killed, and half the human population died. Those who survived had no agricultural stocks to see them through the crisis. Unpaid balances of revenue mounted.

How did cultivators live through such years? How did they pay the revenue, procure their consumption needs, purchase their ploughs and cattle, or get their children married?

Inevitably, they borrowed. Revenue could rarely be paid without a loan from a moneylender. But once a loan was taken, the *ryot* found it difficult to pay it back. As debt mounted, and loans remained unpaid, peasants' dependence on moneylenders increased. They now needed loans even to buy their everyday needs and meet their production expenditure. By the 1840s, officials were finding evidence of alarming levels of peasant indebtedness everywhere.

By the mid-1840s there were signs of an economic recovery of sorts. Many British officials had begun to realise that the settlements of the 1820s had been harsh. The revenue demanded was exorbitant, the system rigid, and the peasant economy on the verge of collapse. So the revenue demand was moderated to encourage peasants to expand cultivation. After 1845 agricultural prices recovered steadily. Cultivators were now extending their acreage, moving into new areas, and transforming pastureland into cultivated fields. But to expand cultivation peasants needed more ploughs and cattle. They needed money to buy seeds and land. For all this they had to turn once again to moneylenders for loans.

3.4 Then came the cotton boom

Before the 1860s, three-fourths of raw cotton imports into Britain came from America. British cotton manufacturers had for long been worried about this dependence on American supplies. What would happen if this source was cut off? Troubled by this question, they eagerly looked for alternative sources of supply.

In 1857 the Cotton Supply Association was founded in Britain, and in 1859 the Manchester Cotton Company was formed. Their objective was "to encourage cotton production in every part of the world

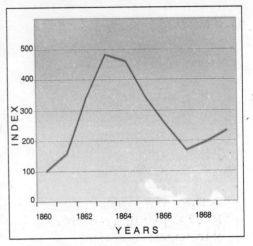

Fig. 10.15
The cotton boom
The line in the graph indicates the rise and fall in cotton prices.

Fig. 10.16
Carts transporting cotton halting under a banyan tree,
Illustrated London News,
13 December 1862

suited for its growth". India was seen as a country that could supply cotton to Lancashire if the American supply dried up. It possessed suitable soil, a climate favourable to cotton cultivation, and cheap labour.

When the American Civil War broke out in 1861, a wave of panic spread through cotton circles in Britain. Raw cotton imports from America fell to less than three per cent of the normal: from over 2,000,000 bales (of 400 lbs each) in 1861 to 55,000 bales in 1862. Frantic messages were sent to India and elsewhere to increase cotton exports to Britain. In Bombay, cotton merchants visited the cotton districts to assess supplies and encourage cultivation. As cotton prices soared (see Fig. 10.15), export merchants in Bombay were keen to secure as much cotton as possible to meet the British demand. So they gave advances to urban *sahukars* who in turn extended credit to those rural moneylenders who promised to secure the produce. When there is a boom in the market credit flows easily, for those who give out loans feel secure about recovering their money.

> ➲ The three panels in Fig. 10.17 depict different modes of transporting cotton. Notice the bullocks collapsing under the weight of the cotton, the boulders on the road, and the huge pile of bales on the boat. What is the artist suggesting through these images?

Fig. 10.17
Transporting cotton before the railway era, Illustrated London News, *20 April 1861*
When cotton supplies from America were cut off during the Civil War, Britain hoped that India would supply all the cotton that British industries needed. It began assessing the supply, examining the quality of cotton and studying the methods of production and marketing. This interest was reflected in the pages of the *Illustrated London News*.

These developments had a profound impact on the Deccan countryside. The *ryots* in the Deccan villages suddenly found access to seemingly limitless credit. They were being given Rs 100 as advance for every acre they planted with cotton. *Sahukars* were more than willing to extend long-term loans.

While the American crisis continued, cotton production in the Bombay Deccan expanded. Between 1860 and 1864 cotton acreage doubled. By 1862 over 90 per cent of cotton imports into Britain were coming from India.

But these boom years did not bring prosperity to all cotton producers. Some rich peasants did gain, but for the large majority, cotton expansion meant heavier debt.

Fig. 10.18
A fleet of boats carrying cotton bales down the Ganges from Mirzapur, Illustrated London News, *13 December 1862*
Before the railway age, the town of Mirzapur was a collection centre for cotton from the Deccan.

Fig. 10.19
Cotton bales lying at the Bombay terminus of the Great Indian Peninsula Railway ready for shipment to England, Illustrated London News, *23 August 1862*
Once the railways came up cotton supplies were not carried only on carts and boats. River traffic declined over time. But older modes of transport were not fully displaced. The loaded bullock cart in the foreground on the right is waiting to carry cotton bales from the railway station to the port.

3.5 Credit dries up

While the boom lasted, cotton merchants in India had visions of capturing the world market in raw cotton, permanently displacing America. The editor of the *Bombay Gazette* had asked in 1861, "What can prevent India from supplanting the Slave States (of U.S.A.) as the feeder of Lancashire?" By 1865 these dreams were over. As the Civil War ended, cotton production in America revived and Indian cotton exports to Britain steadily declined.

Export merchants and *sahukars* in Maharashtra were no longer keen on extending long-term credit. They could see the demand for Indian cotton fall and cotton prices slide downwards. So they decided to close down their operations, restrict their advances to peasants, and demand repayment of outstanding debts.

While credit dried up, the revenue demand increased. The first revenue settlement, as we have seen, was in the 1820s and 1830s. Now it was time for the next. And in the new settlement, the demand was increased dramatically: from 50 to 100 per cent. How could *ryots* pay this inflated demand at a time when prices were falling and cotton fields disappearing? Yet again they had to turn to the moneylender. But the moneylender now refused loans. He no longer had confidence in the *ryots'* capacity to repay.

3.6 The experience of injustice

The refusal of moneylenders to extend loans enraged the *ryots*. What infuriated them was not simply that they had got deeper and deeper into debt, or that they were utterly dependent on the moneylender for survival, but that moneylenders were being insensitive to their plight. The moneylenders were violating the customary norms of the countryside.

Moneylending was certainly widespread before colonial rule and moneylenders were often powerful

Source 8

A ryot petitions

This is an example of a petition from a *ryot* of the village of Mirajgaon, Taluka Karjat, to the Collector, Ahmednagar, Deccan Riots Commission:

The *sowkars* (*sahukars*) ... have of late begun to oppress us. As we cannot earn enough to defray our household expenses, we are actually forced to beg of them to provide us with money, clothes and grain, which we obtain from them not without great difficulty, nor without their compelling us to enter into hard conditions in the bond. Moreover the necessary clothes and grain are not sold to us at cash rates. The prices asked from us are generally twenty-five or fifty per cent more than demanded from customers making ready money payments ... The produce of our fields is also taken by the *sowkars*, who at the time of removing it assure us that it will be credited to our account, but they do not actually make any mention of it in the accounts. They also refuse to pass us any receipts for the produce so removed by them.

⟳ Explain the complaints that the *ryot* is making in the petition. Why was the harvest taken by the moneylenders not credited to the peasants' account? Why were peasants not given any receipts? If you were a moneylender what reasons would you give for these practices?

figures. A variety of customary norms regulated the relationship between the moneylender and the *ryot*. One general norm was that the interest charged could not be more than the principal. This was meant to limit the moneylender's exactions and defined what could be counted as "fair interest". Under colonial rule this norm broke down. In one of the many cases investigated by the Deccan Riots Commission, the moneylender had charged over Rs 2,000 as interest on a loan of Rs 100. In petition after petition, *ryots* complained of the injustice of such exactions and the violation of custom.

Source 9

Deeds of hire

When debts mounted the peasant was unable to pay back the loan to the moneylender. He had no option but to give over all his possessions – land, carts, and animals – to the moneylender. But without animals he could not continue to cultivate. So he took land on rent and animals on hire. He now had to pay for the animals which had originally belonged to him. He had to sign a deed of hire stating very clearly that these animals and carts did not belong to him. In cases of conflict, these deeds could be enforced through the court.

The following is the text of a deed that a peasant signed in November 1873, from the records of the Deccan Riots Commission:

I have sold to you, on account of the debt due to you, my two carriages having iron axles, with their appurtenances and four bullocks ... I have taken from you on hire under (this) deed the very same two carriages and four bullocks. I shall pay every month the hire thereof at Rupees four a month, and obtain a receipt in your own handwriting. In the absence of a receipt I shall not contend that the hire had been paid.

➲ List all the commitments that the peasant is making in this deed. What does such a deed of hire tell us about the relationship between the peasant and the moneylender? How would it change the relationship between the peasant and the bullocks he previously owned?

The *ryots* came to see the moneylender as devious and deceitful. They complained of moneylenders manipulating laws and forging accounts. In 1859 the British passed a Limitation Law that stated that the loan bonds signed between moneylenders and *ryots* would have validity for only three years. This law was meant to check the accumulation of interest over time. The moneylender, however, turned the law around, forcing the *ryot* to sign a new bond every three years. When a new bond was signed, the unpaid balance – that is, the original loan and the accumulated interest – was entered as the principal on which a new set of interest charges was calculated. In petitions that the Deccan Riots Commission collected, *ryots* described how this process worked (see Source 10) and how moneylenders used a variety of other means to short-change the *ryot*: they refused to give receipts when loans were repaid, entered fictitious figures in bonds, acquired the peasants' harvest at low prices, and ultimately took over peasants' property.

Deeds and bonds appeared as symbols of the new oppressive system. In the past such deeds had been rare. The British, however, were suspicious of transactions based on informal understanding, as was common in the past. The terms of transactions, they believed, had to be clearly, unambiguously and categorically stated in contracts, deeds and bonds, and regulated by law. Unless the deed or contract was legally enforceable, it had no value.

Over time, peasants came to associate the misery of their lives with the new regime of bonds and deeds. They were made to sign and put thumb impressions on documents, but they did not know what they were actually signing. They had no idea of the clauses that moneylenders inserted in the bonds. They feared the written word. But they had no choice because to survive they needed loans, and moneylenders were unwilling to give loans without legal bonds.

Source 10

How debts mounted

In a petition to the Deccan Riots Commission a *ryot* explained how the system of loans worked:

A *sowkar* lends his debtor Rs 100 on bond at Rs 3-2 annas per cent per mensem. The latter agrees to pay the amount within eight days from the passing of the bond. Three years after the stipulated time for repaying the amount, the *sowkar* takes from his debtor another bond for the principal and interest together at the same rate of interest, and allows him 125 days' time to liquidate the debt. After the lapse of 3 years and 15 days a third bond is passed by the debtor ... (this process is repeated) at the end of 12 years ... his interest on Rs 1000 amounts to Rs 2028 -10 annas -3 paise.

➲ Calculate the rate of interest that the *ryot* was paying over the years.

4. THE DECCAN RIOTS COMMISSION

When the revolt spread in the Deccan, the Government of Bombay was initially unwilling to see it as anything serious. But the Government of India, worried by the memory of 1857, pressurised the Government of Bombay to set up a commission of enquiry to investigate into the causes of the riots. The commission produced a report that was presented to the British Parliament in 1878.

This report, referred to as the Deccan Riots Report, provides historians with a range of sources for the study of the riot. The commission held enquiries in the districts where the riots spread, recorded statements of *ryots, sahukars* and eyewitnesses, compiled statistical data on revenue rates, prices and interest rates in different regions, and collated the reports sent by district collectors.

In looking at such sources we have to again remember that they are official sources and reflect official concerns and interpretations of events. The Deccan Riots Commission, for instance, was specifically asked to judge whether the level of government revenue demand was the cause of the revolt. And after presenting all the evidence, the commission reported that the government demand was not the cause of peasant anger. It was the moneylenders who were to blame. This argument is found very frequently in colonial records. This shows that there was a persistent reluctance on the part of the colonial government to admit that popular discontent was ever on account of government action.

Official reports, thus, are invaluable sources for the reconstruction of history. But they have to be always read with care and juxtaposed with evidence culled from newspapers, unofficial accounts, legal records and, where possible, oral sources.

⊃ Discuss...

Check what rates of interest are charged in the region where you live at present. Find out whether these rates have changed over the last 50 years. Is there a variation in the rates paid by different groups of people? What are the reasons for the differences?

TIMELINE

1765	English East India Company acquires Diwani of Bengal
1773	Regulating Act passed by the British Parliament to regulate the activities of the East India Company
1793	Permanent Settlement in Bengal
1800s	Santhals begin to come to the Rajmahal hills and settle there
1818	First revenue settlement in the Bombay Deccan
1820s	Agricultural prices begin to fall
1840s-50s	A slow process of agrarian expansion in the Bombay Deccan
1855-56	Santhal rebellion
1861	Cotton boom begins
1875	*Ryots* in Deccan villages rebel

Fig. 10.20
A rural scene, painted by William Prinsep, 1820

ANSWER IN 100-150 WORDS

1. Why was the *jotedar* a powerful figure in many areas of rural Bengal?

2. How did zamindars manage to retain control over their zamindaris?

3. How did the Paharias respond to the coming of outsiders?

4. Why did the Santhals rebel against British rule?

5. What explains the anger of the Deccan *ryots* against the moneylenders?

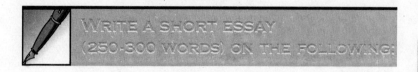

WRITE A SHORT ESSAY
(250-300 WORDS) ON THE FOLLOWING:

6. Why were many zamindaris auctioned after the Permanent Settlement?

7. In what way was the livelihood of the Paharias different from that of the Santhals?

8. How did the American Civil War affect the lives of *ryots* in India?

9. What are the problems of using official sources in writing about the history of peasants?

MAP WORK

10. On an outline map of the subcontinent, mark out the areas described in this chapter. Find out whether there were other areas where the Permanent Settlement and the *ryotwari* system were prevalent and plot these on the map as well.

PROJECTS (CHOOSE ONE)

11. Francis Buchanan published reports on several districts of eastern India. Read one report and collate the information available about rural society, focusing on the themes discussed in this chapter. Highlight the ways in which historians can use such texts.

12. In the region where you live, talk to the older people within a rural community and visit the fields they now cultivate. Find out what they produce, how they earn their livelihoods, what their parents did, what their sons and daughters do now, and how their lives have changed over the last 75 years. Write a report based on your findings.

If you would like to know more, read:

Sugata Bose. 1986. *Agrarian Bengal.* Cambridge University Press, Cambridge.

Francis Buchanan.1930. *Journal of Francis Buchanan Kept During the Survey of the District of Bhagalpur.* Superintendent, Government Printing, Bihar and Orissa, Patna.

Ramachandra Guha. 1989. *The Unquiet Woods: Ecological Change and Peasant Resistance in the Himalayas.* Oxford University Press, New Delhi.

Sumit Guha. 1985. *The Agrarian Economy of the Bombay Deccan, 1818-1941.* Oxford University Press, New Delhi.

Ravinder Kumar. 1968. *Western India in the Nineteenth Century: A Study in the Social History of Maharashtra.* Routledge and Kegan Paul, London.

Ratnalekha Ray. 1979. *Change in Bengal Agrarian Society,* c. *1760-1850.* Manohar, New Delhi.

Kumar Suresh Singh. 1966. *Dust-storm and the Hanging Mist: A Study of Birsa Munda and His Movement in Chhotanagpur (1874-1901).* Firma K.L. Mukhopadhyay, Calcutta.

REBELS AND THE RAJ
THE REVOLT OF 1857
AND ITS REPRESENTATIONS

Late in the afternoon of 10 May 1857, the sepoys in the cantonment of Meerut broke out in mutiny. It began in the lines of the native infantry, spread very swiftly to the cavalry and then to the city. The ordinary people of the town and surrounding villages joined the sepoys. The sepoys captured the bell of arms where the arms and ammunition were kept and proceeded to attack white people, and to ransack and burn their bungalows and property. Government buildings – the record office, jail, court, post office, treasury, etc. – were destroyed and plundered. The telegraph line to Delhi was cut. As darkness descended, a group of sepoys rode off towards Delhi.

Fig. 11.1
Portrait of Bahadur Shah

The sepoys arrived at the gates of the Red Fort early in the morning on 11 May. It was the month of Ramzan, the Muslim holy month of prayer and fasting. The old Mughal emperor, Bahadur Shah, had just finished his prayers and meal before the sun rose and the fast began. He heard the commotion at the gates. The sepoys who had gathered under his window told him: "We have come from Meerut after killing all the Englishmen there, because they asked us to bite bullets that were coated with the fat of cows and pigs with our teeth. This has corrupted the faith of Hindus and Muslims alike." Another group of sepoys also entered Delhi, and the ordinary people of the city joined them. Europeans were killed in large numbers; the rich of Delhi were attacked and looted. It was clear that Delhi had gone out of British control. Some sepoys rode into the Red Fort, without observing the elaborate court etiquette expected of them. They demanded that the emperor give them his blessings. Surrounded by the sepoys, Bahadur Shah had no other option but to comply. The revolt thus acquired a kind of legitimacy because it could now be carried on in the name of the Mughal emperor.

Through 12 and 13 May, North India remained quiet. Once word spread that Delhi had fallen to the rebels and Bahadur Shah had blessed the rebellion, events moved swiftly. Cantonment after cantonment in the Gangetic valley and some to the west of Delhi rose in mutiny.

1. PATTERN OF THE REBELLION

If one were to place the dates of these mutinies in chronological order, it would appear that as the news of the mutiny in one town travelled to the next the sepoys there took up arms. The sequence of events in every cantonment followed a similar pattern.

Bell of arms is a storeroom in which weapons are kept

1.1 How the mutinies began

The sepoys began their action with a signal: in many places it was the firing of the evening gun or the sounding of the bugle. They first seized the bell of arms and plundered the treasury. They then attacked government buildings – the jail, treasury, telegraph office, record room, bungalows – burning all records. Everything and everybody connected with the white man became a target. Proclamations in Hindi, Urdu and Persian were put up in the cities calling upon the population, both Hindus and Muslims, to unite, rise and exterminate the *firangis*.

Firangi, a term of Persian origin, possibly derived from Frank (from which France gets its name), is used in Urdu and Hindi, often in a derogatory sense, to designate foreigners.

When ordinary people began joining the revolt, the targets of attack widened. In major towns like Lucknow, Kanpur and Bareilly, money-lenders and the rich also became the objects of rebel wrath. Peasants not only saw them as oppressors but also as allies of the British. In most places their houses were looted and destroyed. The mutiny in the sepoy ranks quickly became a rebellion. There was a general defiance of all kinds of authority and hierarchy.

Fig. 11.2
Ordinary people join the sepoys in attacking the British in Lucknow.

In the months of May and June, the British had no answer to the actions of the rebels. Individual Britons tried to save their own lives and the lives of their families. British rule, as one British officer noted, "collapsed like a house made of cards".

Source 1

Ordinary life in extraordinary times

What happened in the cities during the months of the revolt? How did people live through those months of tumult? How was normal life affected? Reports from different cities tell us about the breakdown in routine activities. Read these reports from the *Delhi Urdu Akhbar*, 14 June 1857:

> The same thing is true for vegetables and *saag* (spinach). People have been found to complain that even *kaddu* (pumpkin) and *baingan* (brinjal) cannot be found in the bazaars. Potatoes and *arvi* (yam) when available are of stale and rotten variety, stored from before by farsighted *kunjras* (vegetable growers). From the gardens inside the city some produce does reach a few places but the poor and the middle class can only lick their lips and watch them (as they are earmarked for the select).

> ... There is something else that needs attention which is causing a lot of damage to the people which is that the water-carriers have stopped filling water. Poor *Shurfas* (gentility) are seen carrying water in pails on their shoulders and only then the necessary household tasks such as cooking, etc. can take place. The *halalkhors* (righteous) have become *haramkhors* (corrupt), many *mohallas* have not been able to earn for several days and if this situation continues then decay, death and disease will combine together to spoil the city's air and an epidemic will spread all over the city and even to areas adjacent and around.

➲ Read the two reports and the descriptions of what was happening in Delhi provided in the chapter. Remember that newspaper reports often express the prejudices of the reporter. How did *Delhi Urdu Akhbar* view the actions of the people?

1.2 Lines of communication

The reason for the similarity in the pattern of the revolt in different places lay partly in its planning and coordination. It is clear that there was communication between the sepoy lines of various cantonments. After the 7th Awadh Irregular Cavalry had refused to accept the new cartridges in early May, they wrote to the 48th Native Infantry that "they had acted for the faith and awaited the 48th's orders". Sepoys or their emissaries moved from one station to another. People were thus planning and talking about the rebellion.

Source 2

Sisten and the *tahsildar*

In the context of the communication of the message of revolt and mutiny, the experience of François Sisten, a native Christian police inspector in Sitapur, is telling. He had gone to Saharanpur to pay his respects to the magistrate. Sisten was dressed in Indian clothes and sitting cross-legged. A Muslim *tahsildar* from Bijnor entered the room; upon learning that Sisten was from Awadh, he enquired, "What news from Awadh? How does the work progress, brother?" Playing safe, Sisten replied, "If we have work in Awadh, your highness will know it." The *tahsildar* said, "Depend upon it, we will succeed this time. The direction of the business is in able hands." The *tahsildar* was later identified as the principal rebel leader of Bijnor.

➲ What does this conversation suggest about the ways in which plans were communicated and discussed by the rebels? Why did the *tahsildar* regard Sisten as a potential rebel?

The pattern of the mutinies and the pieces of evidence that suggest some sort of planning and coordination raise certain crucial questions. How were the plans made? Who were the planners? It is difficult on the basis of the available documents to provide direct answers to such questions. But one incident provides clues as to how the mutinies came to be so organised. Captain Hearsey of the Awadh Military Police had been given protection by his Indian subordinates during the mutiny. The 41st Native Infantry, which was stationed in the same place, insisted that since they had killed all their white officers, the Military Police should also kill Hearsey or deliver him as prisoner to the 41st. The Military Police refused to do either, and it was decided that the matter would be settled by a panchayat composed of native officers drawn from each regiment. Charles Ball, who wrote one of the earliest histories of the uprising, noted that panchayats were a nightly occurrence in the Kanpur sepoy lines. What this suggests is that some of the decisions were taken collectively. Given the fact that the sepoys lived in lines and shared a common lifestyle and that many of them came from the same caste, it is not difficult to imagine them sitting together to decide their own future. The sepoys were the makers of their own rebellion.

Mutiny – a collective disobedience of rules and regulations within the armed forces

Revolt – a rebellion of people against established authority and power. The terms 'revolt' and 'rebellion' can be used synonymously.

In the context of the revolt of 1857 the term revolt refers primarily to the uprising of the civilian population (peasants, zamindars, rajas, *jagirdars*) while the mutiny was of the sepoys.

Fig. 11.3
Rani Lakshmi Bai, a popular image

Fig. 11.4
Nana Sahib
At the end of 1858, when the
rebellion collapsed, Nana Sahib
escaped to Nepal. The story of his
escape added to the legend of
Nana Sahib's courage and valour.

1.3 Leaders and followers

To fight the British, leadership and organisation
were required. For these the rebels sometimes
turned to those who had been leaders before the
British conquest. One of the first acts of the
sepoys of Meerut, as we saw, was to rush to Delhi
and appeal to the old Mughal emperor to accept
the leadership of the revolt. This acceptance of
leadership took its time in coming. Bahadur
Shah's first reaction was one of horror and
rejection. It was only when some sepoys had
moved into the Mughal court within the Red Fort,
in defiance of normal court etiquette, that the
old emperor, realising he had very few options,
agreed to be the nominal leader of the rebellion.

Elsewhere, similar scenes were enacted
though on a minor scale. In Kanpur, the sepoys
and the people of the town gave Nana Sahib,
the successor to Peshwa Baji Rao II, no choice
save to join the revolt as their leader. In Jhansi,
the rani was forced by the popular pressure
around her to assume the leadership of the
uprising. So was Kunwar Singh, a local
zamindar in Arrah in Bihar. In Awadh, where
the displacement of the popular Nawab Wajid
Ali Shah and the annexation of the state were
still very fresh in the memory of the people,
the populace in Lucknow celebrated the fall of
British rule by hailing Birjis Qadr, the young
son of the Nawab, as their leader.

Not everywhere were the leaders people of the
court – ranis, rajas, nawabs and *taluqdars*.
Often the message of rebellion was carried by
ordinary men and women and in places by
religious men too. From Meerut, there were
reports that a fakir had appeared riding on an
elephant and that the sepoys were visiting him
frequently. In Lucknow, after the annexation of
Awadh, there were many religious leaders and
self-styled prophets who preached the
destruction of British rule.

Elsewhere, local leaders emerged, urging
peasants, zamindars and tribals to revolt. Shah
Mal mobilised the villagers of pargana Barout in
Uttar Pradesh; Gonoo, a tribal cultivator of
Singhbhum in Chotanagpur, became a rebel
leader of the Kol tribals of the region.

Two rebels of 1857

Shah Mal

Shah Mal lived in a large village in pargana Barout in Uttar Pradesh. He belonged to a clan of Jat cultivators whose kinship ties extended over *chaurasee des* (eighty-four villages). The lands in the region were irrigated and fertile, with rich dark loam soil. Many of the villagers were prosperous and saw the British land revenue system as oppressive: the revenue demand was high and its collection inflexible. Consequently cultivators were losing land to outsiders, to traders and moneylenders who were coming into the area.

Shah Mal mobilised the headmen and cultivators of *chaurasee des*, moving at night from village to village, urging people to rebel against the British. As in many other places, the revolt against the British turned into a general rebellion against all signs of oppression and injustice. Cultivators left their fields and plundered the houses of moneylenders and traders. Displaced proprietors took possession of the lands they had lost. Shah Mal's men attacked government buildings, destroyed the bridge over the river, and dug up metalled roads – partly to prevent government forces from coming into the area, and partly because bridges and roads were seen as symbols of British rule. They sent supplies to the sepoys who had mutinied in Delhi and stopped all official communication between British headquarters and Meerut. Locally acknowledged as the Raja, Shah Mal took over the bungalow of an English officer, turned it into a "hall of justice", settling disputes and dispensing judgments. He also set up an amazingly effective network of intelligence. For a period the people of the area felt that *firangi raj* was over, and their *raj* had come.

Shah Mal was killed in battle in July 1857.

Maulvi Ahmadullah Shah

Maulvi Ahmadullah Shah was one of the many *maulvis* who played an important part in the revolt of 1857. Educated in Hyderabad, he became a preacher when young. In 1856, he was seen moving from village to village preaching *jehad* (religious war) against the British and urging people to rebel. He moved in a palanquin, with drumbeaters in front and followers at the rear. He was therefore popularly called Danka Shah – the *maulvi* with the drum (*danka*). British officials panicked as thousands began following the *maulvi* and many Muslims began seeing him as an inspired prophet. When he reached Lucknow in 1856, he was stopped by the police from preaching in the city. Subsequently, in 1857, he was jailed in Faizabad. When released, he was elected by the mutinous 22nd Native Infantry as their leader. He fought in the famous Battle of Chinhat in which the British forces under Henry Lawrence were defeated. He came to be known for his courage and power. Many people in fact believed that he was invincible, had magical powers, and could not be killed by the British. It was this belief that partly formed the basis of his authority.

Fig. 11.5
Henry Hardinge, by Francis Grant,
1849
As Governor General, Hardinge
attempted to modernise the
equipment of the army. The Enfield
rifles that were introduced initially
used the greased cartridges the
sepoys rebelled against.

1.4 Rumours and prophecies

Rumours and prophecies played a part in moving
people to action. As we saw, the sepoys who had
arrived in Delhi from Meerut had told Bahadur Shah
about bullets coated with the fat of cows and pigs
and that biting those bullets would corrupt their
caste and religion. They were referring to the
cartridges of the Enfield rifles which had just been
given to them. The British tried to explain to the
sepoys that this was not the case but the rumour
that the new cartridges were greased with the fat of
cows and pigs spread like wildfire across the sepoy
lines of North India.

This is one rumour whose origin can be traced.
Captain Wright, commandant of the Rifle Instruction
Depot, reported that in the third week of January
1857 a "low-caste" *khalasi* who worked in the
magazine in Dum Dum had asked a Brahmin sepoy
for a drink of water from his *lota*. The sepoy had
refused saying that the "lower caste's" touch would
defile the *lota*. The *khalasi* had reportedly retorted,
"You will soon lose your caste, as ere long you will
have to bite cartridges covered with the fat of cows
and pigs." We do not know the veracity of the report,
but once this rumour started no amount of
assurances from British officers could stop its
circulation and the fear it spread among the sepoys.

This was not the only rumour that was circulating
in North India at the beginning of 1857. There was
the rumour that the British government had hatched
a gigantic conspiracy to destroy the caste and religion
of Hindus and Muslims. To this end, the rumours
said, the British had mixed the bone dust of cows
and pigs into the flour that was sold in the market.
In towns and cantonments, sepoys and the common
people refused to touch the *atta*. There was fear and
suspicion that the British wanted to convert Indians
to Christianity. Panic spread fast. British officers
tried to allay their fears, but in vain. These fears
stirred men to action. The response to the call for
action was reinforced by the prophecy that British
rule would come to an end on the centenary of the
Battle of Plassey, on 23 June 1857.

Rumours were not the only thing circulating at
the time. Reports came from various parts of North
India that chapattis were being distributed from
village to village. A person would come at night and

give a chapatti to the watchman of the village and ask him to make five more and distribute to the next village, and so on. The meaning and purpose of the distribution of the chapattis was not clear and is not clear even today. But there is no doubt that people read it as an omen of an upheaval.

1.5 Why did people believe in the rumours?

We cannot understand the power of rumours and prophecies in history by checking whether they are factually correct or not. We need to see what they reflect about the minds of people who believed them – their fears and apprehensions, their faiths and convictions. Rumours circulate only when they resonate with the deeper fears and suspicions of people.

The rumours in 1857 begin to make sense when seen in the context of the policies the British pursued from the late 1820s. As you know, from that time, under the leadership of Governor General Lord William Bentinck, the British adopted policies aimed at "reforming" Indian society by introducing Western education, Western ideas and Western institutions. With the cooperation of sections of Indian society they set up English-medium schools, colleges and universities which taught Western sciences and the liberal arts. The British established laws to abolish customs like sati (1829) and to permit the remarriage of Hindu widows.

On a variety of pleas, like misgovernment and the refusal to recognise adoption, the British annexed not only Awadh, but many other kingdoms and principalities like Jhansi and Satara. Once these territories were annexed, the British introduced their own system of administration, their own laws and their own methods of land settlement and land revenue collection. The cumulative impact of all this on the people of North India was profound.

It seemed to the people that all that they cherished and held sacred – from kings and socio-religious customs to patterns of landholding and revenue payment – was being destroyed and replaced by a system that was more impersonal, alien and oppressive. This perception was aggravated by the activities of Christian missionaries. In such a situation of uncertainty, rumours spread with remarkable swiftness.

To explore the basis of the revolt of 1857 in some detail, let us look at Awadh – one of the major centres where the drama of 1857 unfolded.

⊃ Discuss...
Read the section once more and explain the similarities and differences you notice in the ways in which leaders emerged during the revolt. For any two leaders, discuss why ordinary people were drawn to them.

2. AWADH IN REVOLT

2.1 "A cherry that will drop into our mouth one day"

In 1851 Governor General Lord Dalhousie described the kingdom of Awadh as "a cherry that will drop into our mouth one day". Five years later, in 1856, the kingdom was formally annexed to the British Empire.

The conquest happened in stages. The Subsidiary Alliance had been imposed on Awadh in 1801. By the terms of this alliance the Nawab had to disband his military force, allow the British to position their troops within the kingdom, and act in accordance with the advice of the British Resident who was now to be attached to the court. Deprived of his armed forces, the Nawab became increasingly dependent on the British to maintain law and order within the kingdom. He could no longer assert control over the rebellious chiefs and *taluqdars*.

In the meantime the British became increasingly interested in acquiring the territory of Awadh. They felt that the soil there was good for producing indigo and cotton, and the region was ideally located to be developed into the principal market of Upper India. By the early 1850s, moreover, all the major areas of India had been conquered: the Maratha lands, the Doab, the Carnatic, the Punjab and Bengal. The takeover of Awadh in 1856 was expected to complete a process of territorial annexation that had begun with the conquest of Bengal almost a century earlier.

2.2 "The life was gone out of the body"

Lord Dalhousie's annexations created disaffection in all the areas and principalities that were annexed but nowhere more so than in the kingdom of Awadh in the heart of North India. Here, Nawab Wajid Ali Shah was dethroned and exiled to Calcutta on the plea that the region was being misgoverned. The British government also wrongly assumed that Wajid Ali Shah was an unpopular ruler. On the contrary, he was widely loved, and when he left his beloved Lucknow, there were many who followed him all the way to Kanpur singing songs of lament.

The widespread sense of grief and loss at the Nawab's exile was recorded by many contemporary observers. One of them wrote: "The life was gone out of the body, and the body of this town had been left lifeless ... there was no street or market and house

Resident was the designation of a representative of the Governor General who lived in a state which was not under direct British rule.

Subsidiary Alliance

Subsidiary Alliance was a system devised by Lord Wellesley in 1798. All those who entered into such an alliance with the British had to accept certain terms and conditions:

(a) The British would be responsible for protecting their ally from external and internal threats to their power.

(b) In the territory of the ally, a British armed contingent would be stationed.

(c) The ally would have to provide the resources for maintaining this contingent.

(d) The ally could enter into agreements with other rulers or engage in warfare only with the permission of the British.

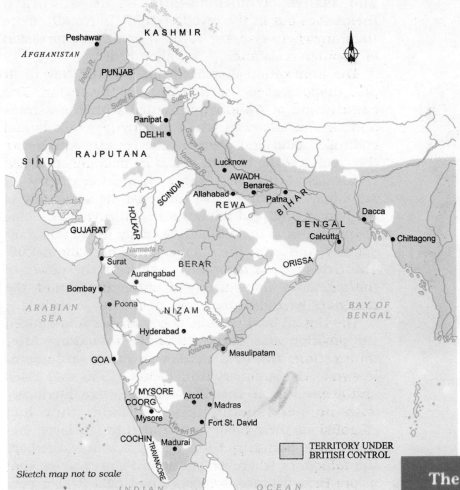

Map 1
Territories under British control in 1857

Sketch map not to scale

TERRITORY UNDER
BRITISH CONTROL

which did not wail out the cry of agony in separation
of Jan-i-Alam." One folk song bemoaned that "the
honourable English came and took the country"
(*Angrez Bahadur ain, mulk lai linho*).

This emotional upheaval was aggravated by
immediate material losses. The removal of the Nawab
led to the dissolution of the court and its culture.
Thus a whole range of people – musicians, dancers,
poets, artisans, cooks, retainers, administrative
officials and so on – lost their livelihood.

2.3 *Firangi raj* and the end of a world

A chain of grievances in Awadh linked prince,
taluqdar, peasant and sepoy. In different ways they
came to identify *firangi raj* with the end of their
world – the breakdown of things they valued,
respected and held dear. A whole complex of emotions

Source 3

The Nawab has left

Another song mourned the
plight of the ruler who had to
leave his motherland:

Noble and peasant all wept
together

and all the world wept and
wailed

Alas! The chief has bidden
adieu to

his country and gone
abroad.

➲ Read the entire section
and discuss why people
mourned the departure of
Wajid Ali Shah.

Fig. 11.6
A zamindar from Awadh, 1880

and issues, traditions and loyalties worked themselves out in the revolt of 1857. In Awadh, more than anywhere else, the revolt became an expression of popular resistance to an alien order.

The annexation displaced not just the Nawab. It also dispossessed the *taluqdars* of the region. The countryside of Awadh was dotted with the estates and forts of *taluqdars* who for many generations had controlled land and power in the countryside. Before the coming of the British, *taluqdars* maintained armed retainers, built forts, and enjoyed a degree of autonomy, as long as they accepted the suzerainty of the Nawab and paid the revenue of their *taluqs*. Some of the bigger *taluqdars* had as many as 12,000 foot-soldiers and even the smaller ones had about 200. The British were unwilling to tolerate the power of the *taluqdars*. Immediately after the annexation, the *taluqdars* were disarmed and their forts destroyed.

The British land revenue policy further undermined the position and authority of the *taluqdars*. After annexation, the first British revenue settlement, known as the Summary Settlement of 1856, was based on the assumption that the *taluqdars* were interlopers with no permanent stakes in land: they had established their hold over land through force and fraud. The Summary Settlement proceeded to remove the *taluqdars* wherever possible. Figures show that in pre-British times, *taluqdars* had held 67 per cent of the total number of villages in Awadh; by the Summary Settlement this number had come down to 38 per cent. The *taluqdars* of southern Awadh were the hardest hit and some lost more than half of the total number of villages they had previously held.

British land revenue officers believed that by removing *taluqdars* they would be able to settle the land with the actual owners of the soil and thus reduce the level of exploitation of peasants while increasing revenue returns for the state. But this did not happen in practice: revenue flows for the state increased but the burden of demand on the peasants did not decline. Officials soon found that large areas of Awadh were actually heavily overassessed: the increase of revenue demand in some places was from 30 to 70 per cent. Thus neither *taluqdars* nor peasants had any reasons to be happy with the annexation.

The dispossession of *taluqdars* meant the breakdown of an entire social order. The ties of loyalty and patronage that had bound the peasant to the *taluqdar* were disrupted. In pre-British times, the *taluqdars* were oppressors but many of them also appeared to be generous father figures: they exacted a variety of dues from the peasant but were often considerate in times of need. Now, under the British, the peasant was directly exposed to overassessment of revenue and inflexible methods of collection. There was no longer any guarantee that in times of hardship or crop failure the revenue demand of the state would be reduced or collection postponed; or that in times of festivities the peasant would get the loan and support that the *taluqdar* had earlier provided.

In areas like Awadh where resistance during 1857 was intense and long lasting, the fighting was carried out by *taluqdars* and their peasants. Many of these *taluqdars* were loyal to the Nawab of Awadh, and they joined Begum Hazrat Mahal (the wife of the Nawab) in Lucknow to fight the British; some even remained with her in defeat.

The grievances of the peasants were carried over into the sepoy lines since a vast majority of the sepoys were recruited from the villages of Awadh. For decades the sepoys had complained of low levels of pay and the difficulty of getting leave. By the 1850s there were other reasons for their discontent.

The relationship of the sepoys with their superior white officers underwent a significant change in the years preceding the uprising of 1857. In the 1820s, white officers made it a point to maintain friendly relations with the sepoys. They would take part in their leisure activities – they wrestled with them, fenced with them and went out hawking with them. Many of them were fluent in Hindustani and were familiar with the customs and culture of the country. These officers were disciplinarian and father figure rolled into one.

In the 1840s, this began to change. The officers developed a sense of superiority and started treating the sepoys as their racial inferiors, riding roughshod over their sensibilities. Abuse and physical violence became common and thus the distance between sepoys and officers grew. Trust was replaced by suspicion. The episode of the greased cartridges was a classic example of this.

Source 4

What *taluqdars* thought

The attitude of the *taluqdars* was best expressed by Hanwant Singh, the Raja of Kalakankar, near Rae Bareli. During the mutiny, Hanwant Singh had given shelter to a British officer, and conveyed him to safety. While taking leave of the officer, Hanwant Singh told him:

Sahib, your countrymen came into this country and drove out our King. You sent your officers round the districts to examine the titles to the estates. At one blow you took from me lands which from time immemorial had been in my family. I submitted. Suddenly misfortune fell upon you. The people of the land rose against you. You came to me whom you had despoiled. I have saved you. But now – now I march at the head of my retainers to Lucknow to try and drive you from the country.

⮌ What does this excerpt tell you about the attitude of the *taluqdars*? Who did Hanwant Singh mean by the people of the land? What reason does Hanwant Singh give for the anger of the people?

Fig. 11.7
Bengal sepoys in European-style uniform

⊃ Discuss...

Find out whether people in your state participated in the revolt of 1857. If they did, find out why they did so. If they did not, try and explain this.

It is also important to remember that close links existed between the sepoys and the rural world of North India. The large majority of the sepoys of the Bengal Army were recruited from the villages of Awadh and eastern Uttar Pradesh. Many of them were Brahmins or from the "upper" castes. Awadh was, in fact, called the "nursery of the Bengal Army". The changes that the families of the sepoys saw around them and the threats they perceived were quickly transmitted to the sepoy lines. In turn, the fears of the sepoys about the new cartridge, their grievances about leave, their grouse about the increasing misbehaviour and racial abuse on the part of their white officers were communicated back to the villages. This link between the sepoys and the rural world had important implications in the course of the uprising. When the sepoys defied their superior officers and took up arms they were joined very swiftly by their brethren in the villages. Everywhere, peasants poured into towns and joined the soldiers and the ordinary people of the towns in collective acts of rebellion.

3. WHAT THE REBELS WANTED

As victors, the British recorded their own trials and tribulations as well as their heroism. They dismissed the rebels as a bunch of ungrateful and barbaric people. The repression of the rebels also meant silencing of their voice. Few rebels had the opportunity of recording their version of events. Moreover, most of them were sepoys and ordinary people who were not literate. Thus, other than a few proclamations and *ishtahars* (notifications) issued by rebel leaders to propagate their ideas and persuade people to join the revolt, we do not have much that throws light on the perspective of the rebels. Attempts to reconstruct what happened in 1857 are thus heavily and inevitably dependent on what the British wrote. While these sources reveal the minds of officials, they tell us very little about what the rebels wanted.

3.1 The vision of unity

The rebel proclamations in 1857 repeatedly appealed to all sections of the population, irrespective of their caste and creed. Many of the proclamations were issued by Muslim princes or in their names but even these took care to address the sentiments of Hindus. The rebellion was seen as a war in which both Hindus and Muslims had equally to lose or gain. The *ishtahars* harked back to the pre-British Hindu-Muslim past and glorified the coexistence of different communities under the Mughal Empire. The proclamation that was issued under the name of Bahadur Shah appealed to the people to join the fight under the standards of both Muhammad and Mahavir. It was remarkable that during the uprising religious divisions between Hindus and Muslim were hardly noticeable despite British attempts to create such divisions. In Bareilly in western Uttar Pradesh, in December 1857, the British spent Rs 50,000 to incite the Hindu population against the Muslims. The attempt failed.

Source 5

The Azamgarh Proclamation, 25 August 1857

This is one of the main sources of our knowledge about what the rebels wanted:

It is well known to all, that in this age the people of Hindostan, both Hindoos and Mohammedans, are being ruined under the tyranny and the oppression of the infidel and treacherous English. It is therefore the bounden duty of all the wealthy people of India, especially those who have any sort of connection with the Mohammedan royal families, and are considered the pastors and masters of their people, to stake their lives and property for the well-being of the public. ...

Several of the Hindoo and Mussalman Chiefs, who have long since quitted their homes for the preservation of their religion, and have been trying their best to root out the English in India, have presented themselves to me, and taken part in the reigning Indian crusade, and it is more than probable that I shall very shortly receive succours from the West. Therefore for the information of the public, the present *Ishtahar,* consisting of several sections, is put in circulation and it is the imperative duty of all to take into their careful consideration, and abide by it. Parties anxious to participate in the common cause, but having no means to provide for themselves, shall receive their daily subsistence from me; and be it known to all, that the ancient works, both of the Hindoos and Mohammedans, the writings of miracle workers, and the calculation of the astrologers, pundits, ... all agree in asserting that the English will no longer have any footing in India or elsewhere. Therefore it is incumbent on all to give up the hope of the continuation of the British sway, side with me, and deserve the consideration of the Badshahi, or imperial government, by their individual exertion in

contd

Source 5 (contd)

promoting the common good, and thus attain their respective ends; otherwise if this golden opportunity slips away, they will have to repent for their folly, … .

Section I – Regarding Zemindars. It is evident, that the British Government in making zemindary settlements have imposed exorbitant *Jumas* (revenue demand) and have disgraced and ruined several zemindars, by putting up their estates for public auction for arrears of rent, in so much, in the institution of a suit by a common Ryot, a maid servant, or a slave, the respectable zemindars are summoned into court, arrested, put in goal and disgraced. In litigation regarding zemindaries, the immense value of stamps, and other unnecessary expenses of the civil courts, … are all calculated to impoverish the litigants. Besides this, the coffers of the zemindars are annually taxed with the subscription for schools, hospitals, roads, etc. Such extortions will have no manner of existence in the Badshahi Government; but on the contrary the *Jumas* will be light, the dignity and honour of the zemindars safe, and every zemindar will have absolute rule in his own zemindary …

Section II – Regarding Merchants. It is plain that the infidel and treacherous British Government have monopolised the trade of all the fine and valuable merchandise, such as indigo, cloth, and other articles of shipping, leaving only the trade of trifles to the people, … Besides this, the profits of the traders are taxed, with postages, tolls and subscriptions for schools, etc. Notwithstanding all these concessions, the merchants are liable to imprisonment and disgrace at the instance or complaint of a worthless man. When the Badshahi Government is established all these aforesaid fraudulent practices shall be dispensed with, and the trade of every article, without exception, both by land and water will be opened to the native merchants of India, … It is therefore the duty of every merchant to take part in the war, and aid the Badshahi Government with his men and money, … .

Section III – Regarding Public Servants. It is not a secret thing, that under the British Government, natives employed in the civil and military services have little respect, low pay, and no manner of influence; and all the posts of dignity and emolument in both the departments are exclusively bestowed on Englishmen, … Therefore, all the natives in the British service ought to be alive to their religion and interest, and abjuring their loyalty to the English, side with the Badshahi Government, and obtain salaries of 200 and 300 rupees a month for the present, and be entitled to high posts in the future. …

Section IV – Regarding Artisans. It is evident that the Europeans, by the introduction of English articles into India, have thrown the weavers, the cotton dressers, the carpenters, the blacksmiths, and the shoemakers, etc., out of employ, and have engrossed their occupations, so that every description of native artisan has been reduced to beggary. But under the Badshahi Government the native artisans will exclusively be employed in the service of the kings, the rajahs, and the rich; and this will no doubt ensure their prosperity. Therefore these artisans ought to renounce the English services, … .

Section V – Regarding Pundits, Fakirs and Other Learned Persons. The pundits and fakirs being the guardians of the Hindoo and Mohammadan religions respectively, and the Europeans being the enemies of both the religions, and as at present a war is raging against the English on account of religion, the pundits and fakirs are bound to present themselves to me, and take their share in the holy war… .

> ➲ What are the issues against British rule highlighted in this proclamation? Read the section on each social group carefully. Notice the language in which the proclamation is formulated and the variety of sentiments it appeals to.

Source 6

What the sepoys thought

This is one of the *arzis* (petition or application) of rebel sepoys that have survived:

A century ago the British arrived in Hindostan and gradually entertained troops in their service, and became masters of every state. Our forefathers have always served them, and we also entered their service ... By the mercy of God and with our assistance the British also conquered every place they liked, in which thousands of us, Hindostani men were sacrificed, but we never made any excuses or pretences nor revolted ...

But in the year eighteen fifty seven the British issued an order that new cartridges and muskets which had arrived from England were to be issued; in the former of which the fats of cows and pigs were mixed; and also that *attah* of wheat mixed with powdered bones was to be eaten; and even distributed them in every Regiment of infantry, cavalry and artillery ...

They gave these cartridges to the *sowars* (mounted soldiers) of the 3rd Light Cavalry, and ordered them to bite them; the troopers objected to it, and said that they would never bite them, for if they did, their religion and faith would be destroyed ... upon this the British officers paraded the men of the 3 Regiments and having prepared 1,400 English soldiers, and other Battalions of European troops and Horse Artillery, surrounded them, and placing six guns before each of the infantry regiments, loaded the guns with grape and made 84 new troopers prisoners, and put them in jail with irons on them ... The reason that the *sowars* of the Cantonment were put into jail was that we should be frightened into biting the new cartridges. On this account we and all our country-men having united together, have fought the British for the preservation of our faith ... we have been compelled to make war for two years and the Rajahs and Chiefs who are with us in faith and religion, are still so, and have undergone all sorts of trouble; we have fought for two years in order that our faith and religion may not be polluted. If the religion of a Hindoo or Mussalman is lost, what remains in the world?

⊃ Compare the reasons for the mutiny as stated in the *arzi* with those mentioned by the *taluqdar* (Source 3).

3.2 Against the symbols of oppression

The proclamations completely rejected everything associated with British rule or *firangi raj* as they called it. They condemned the British for the annexations they had carried out and the treaties they had broken. The British, the rebel leaders said, could not be trusted.

What enraged the people was how British land revenue settlements had dispossessed landholders, both big and small, and foreign commerce had driven artisans and weavers to ruin. Every aspect of British rule was attacked and the *firangi* accused of destroying a way of life that was familiar and cherished. The rebels wanted to restore that world.

The proclamations expressed the widespread fear that the British were bent on destroying the caste and religions of Hindus and Muslims and converting them to Christianity – a fear that led people to believe many of the rumours that circulated at the time. People were urged to come together and fight to save their livelihood, their faith, their honour, their identity – a fight which was for the "greater public good".

As noted earlier, in many places the rebellion against the British widened into an attack on all those who were seen as allies of the British or local oppressors. Often the rebels deliberately sought to humiliate the elites of a city. In the villages they burnt account books and ransacked moneylenders' houses. This reflected an attempt to overturn traditional hierarchies, rebel against *all* oppressors. It presents a glimpse of an alternative vision, perhaps of a more egalitarian society. Such visions were not articulated in the proclamations which sought to unify all social groups in the fight against *firangi raj*.

3.3 The search for alternative power

Once British rule had collapsed, the rebels in places like Delhi, Lucknow and Kanpur tried to establish some kind of structure of authority and administration. This was, of course, short-lived but the attempts show that the rebel leadership wanted to restore the pre-British world of the eighteenth century. The leaders went back to the culture of the court. Appointments were made to various posts, arrangements made for the collection of land revenue and the payment of troops, orders issued to stop loot and plunder. Side by side plans were made to fight battles against the British. Chains of command were laid down in the army. In all this the rebels harked back to the eighteenth-century Mughal world – a world that became a symbol of all that had been lost.

The administrative structures established by the rebels were primarily aimed at meeting the demands of war. However, in most cases these structures could not survive the British onslaught. But in Awadh, where resistance to the British lasted longest, plans of counter-attack were being drawn up by the Lucknow court and hierarchies of command were in place as late as the last months of 1857 and the early part of 1858.

⊃ Discuss...
What do you think are the major problems faced by historians in reconstructing the point of view of the rebels?

4. REPRESSION

It is clear from all accounts that we have of 1857 that the British did not have an easy time in putting down the rebellion.

Before sending out troops to reconquer North India, the British passed a series of laws to help them quell the insurgency. By a number of Acts, passed in May and June 1857, not only was the whole of North India put under martial law but military officers and even ordinary Britons were given the power to try and punish Indians suspected of rebellion. In other words, the ordinary processes of law and trial were suspended and it was put out that rebellion would have only one punishment – death.

Armed with these newly enacted special laws and the reinforcements brought in from Britain, the British began the task of suppressing the revolt. They, like the rebels, recognised the symbolic value of Delhi. The British thus mounted a two-pronged attack. One force moved from Calcutta into North India and the other from the Punjab – which was largely peaceful – to reconquer Delhi. British

Source 7

Villagers as rebels

An officer reporting from rural Awadh (spelt as Oude in the following account) noted:

The Oude people are gradually pressing down on the line of communication from the North ... the Oude people are villagers ... these villagers are nearly intangible to Europeans melting away before them and collecting again. The Civil Authorities report these villagers to amount to a very large number of men, with a number of guns.

➲ What, according to this account, were the problems faced by the British in dealing with these villagers?

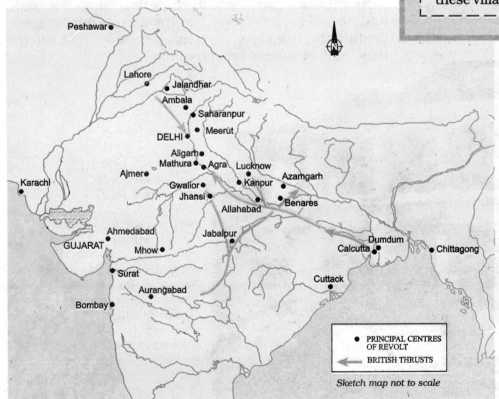

Map 2
The map shows the important centres of revolt and the lines of British attack against the rebels.

PRINCIPAL CENTRES OF REVOLT

BRITISH THRUSTS

Sketch map not to scale

Fig. 11.8
A mosque on the Delhi Ridge,
photograph by Felice Beato, 1857-58
After 1857, British photographers
recorded innumerable images of
desolation and ruin.

attempts to recover Delhi began in earnest in early
June 1857 but it was only in late September that
the city was finally captured. The fighting and losses
on both sides were heavy. One reason for this was
the fact that rebels from all over North India had
come to Delhi to defend the capital.

In the Ganegtic plain too the progress of British
reconquest was slow. The forces had to reconquer
the area village by village. The countryside and the
people around were entirely hostile. As soon as they
began their counter-insurgency operations, the
British realised that they were not dealing with a
mere mutiny but an uprising that had huge popular
support. In Awadh, for example, a British official
called Forsyth estimated that three-fourths of the
adult male population was in rebellion. The area
was brought under control only in March 1858 after
protracted fighting.

The British used military power on a gigantic
scale. But this was not the only instrument they
used. In large parts of present-day Uttar Pradesh,
where big landholders and peasants had offered
united resistance, the British tried to break up the
unity by promising to give back to the big landholders
their estates. Rebel landholders were dispossessed
and the loyal rewarded. Many landholders died
fighting the British or they escaped into Nepal where
they died of illness or starvation.

Fig. 11.9
Secundrah Bagh, Lucknow,
photograph by Felice Beato,
1858
Here we see four solitary
figures within a desolate
place that was once the
pleasure garden built by
Nawab Wajid Ali Shah.
British forces led by
Campbell killed over 2000
rebel sepoys who held the
place in 1857. The skeletons
strewn on the ground are
meant to be a cold warning
of the futility of rebellion.

5. IMAGES OF THE REVOLT

How do we know about the revolt, about the activities of the rebels and the measures of repression that we have been discussing?

As we have seen, we have very few records on the rebels' point of view. There are a few rebel proclamations and notifications, as also some letters that rebel leaders wrote. But historians till now have continued to discuss rebel actions primarily through accounts written by the British.

Official accounts, of course, abound: colonial administrators and military men left their versions in letters and diaries, autobiographies and official histories. We can also gauge the official mindset and the changing British attitudes through the innumerable memos and notes, assessments of situations, and reports that were produced. Many of these have now been collected in a set of volumes on mutiny records. These tell us about the fears and anxieties of officials and their perception of the rebels. The stories of the revolt that were published in British newspapers and magazines narrated in gory detail the violence of the mutineers – and these stories inflamed public feelings and provoked demands of retribution and revenge.

One important record of the mutiny is the pictorial images produced by the British and Indians: paintings, pencil drawings, etchings, posters, cartoons, bazaar prints. Let us look at some of them and see what they tell us.

5.1 Celebrating the saviours

British pictures offer a variety of images that were meant to provoke a range of different emotions and reactions. Some of them commemorate the British heroes who saved the English and repressed the rebels. "Relief of Lucknow", painted by Thomas Jones Barker in 1859, is an example of this type. When the rebel forces besieged Lucknow, Henry Lawrence, the Commissioner of Lucknow, collected the Christian population and took refuge in the heavily fortified Residency. Lawrence was killed but the Residency continued to be defended under the command of Colonel Inglis. On 25 September James Outram and Henry Havelock arrived, cut through the rebel forces, and reinforced the British garrisons. Twenty days later Colin Campbell, who

Fig. 11.10
"Relief of Lucknow", painted by
Thomas Jones Barker, 1859

was appointed as the new Commander of British
forces in India, came with his forces and rescued
the besieged British garrison. In British accounts
the siege of Lucknow became a story of survival,
heroic resistance and the ultimate triumph of
British power.

Barker's painting celebrates the moment of
Campbell's entry. At the centre of the canvas are
the British heroes – Campbell, Outram and Havelock.
The gestures of the hands of those around lead the
spectator's eyes towards the centre. The heroes stand
on a ground that is well lit, with shadows in the
foreground and the damaged Residency in the
background. The dead and injured in the foreground
are testimony to the suffering during the siege, while
the triumphant figures of horses in the middle ground
emphasise the fact that British power and control
had been re-established. To the British public such
paintings were reassuring. They created a sense that
the time of trouble was past and the rebellion was
over; the British were the victors.

5.2 English women and the honour of Britain

Newspaper reports have a power over public
imagination; they shape feelings and attitudes to
events. Inflamed particularly by tales of violence

against women and children, there were public demands in Britain for revenge and retribution. The British government was asked to protect the honour of innocent women and ensure the safety of helpless children. Artists expressed as well as shaped these sentiments through their visual representations of trauma and suffering.

"In Memoriam" (Fig. 11.11) was painted by Joseph Noel Paton two years after the mutiny. You can see English women and children huddled in a circle, looking helpless and innocent, seemingly waiting for the inevitable – dishonour, violence and death. "In Memoriam" does not show gory violence; it only suggests it. It stirs up the spectator's imagination, and seeks to provoke anger and fury. It represents the rebels as violent and brutish, even though they remain invisible in the picture. In the background you can see the British rescue forces arriving as saviours.

Fig. 11.11
"In Memoriam",
by Joseph Noel Paton, 1859

Fig. 11.12
*Miss Wheeler defending herself
against sepoys in Kanpur*

In another set of sketches and paintings we see women in a different light. They appear heroic, defending themselves against the attack of rebels. Miss Wheeler in Figure 11.12 stands firmly at the centre, defending her honour, single-handedly killing the attacking rebels. As in all such British representations, the rebels are demonised. Here, four burly males with swords and guns are shown attacking a woman. The woman's struggle to save her honour and her life, in fact, is represented as having a deeper religious connotation: it is a battle to save the honour of Christianity. The book lying on the floor is the Bible.

5.3 Vengeance and retribution

As waves of anger and shock spread in Britain, demands for retribution grew louder. Visual representations and news about the revolt created a milieu in which violent repression and vengeance were seen as both necessary and just. It was as if justice demanded that the challenge to British honour and power be met ruthlessly. Threatened by the rebellion, the British felt that they had to demonstrate their invincibility. In one such image (Fig. 11.13) we see an allegorical female figure of justice with a sword in one hand and a shield in the other. Her posture is aggressive; her face expresses rage and the desire for revenge. She is trampling sepoys under her feet while a mass of Indian women with children cower with fear.

There were innumerable other pictures and cartoons in the British press that sanctioned brutal repression and violent reprisal.

JUSTICE.

Fig. 11.13
Justice, Punch, *12 September 1857*
The caption at the bottom reads "The news of the terrible massacre at Cawnpore (Kanpur) produced an outburst of fiery indignation and wild desire for revenge throughout the whole of England."

THE BRITISH LION'S VENGEANCE ON THE BENGAL TIGER.

Fig. 11.14
The caption at the bottom reads "The British Lion's Vengeance on the Bengal Tiger", Punch, 1857.

➲ What idea is the picture projecting? What is being expressed through the images of the lion and the tiger? What do the figures of the woman and the child depict?

5.4 The performance of terror

The urge for vengeance and retribution was expressed in the brutal way in which the rebels were executed. They were blown from guns, or hanged from the gallows. Images of these executions were widely circulated through popular journals.

Fig. 11.15
Execution of mutineers in Peshawar: Blowing from the guns,
Illustrated London News, *3 October 1857*
The scene of execution here appears to be a stage where a drama is being performed – an enactment of brutal power. Mounted soldiers and sepoys in uniform dominate the scene. They have to watch the execution of their fellow sepoys, and experience the chilling consequences of rebellion.

Fig. 11.16
Execution of mutinous sepoys in Peshawar, Illustrated London News, *3 October 1857*
In this scene of execution 12 rebels hang in a row, with cannons all around them.
What you see is not routine punishment: it is the performance of terror. For it to instil
fear among people, punishment could not be discreetly meted out in enclosed spaces.
It had to be theatrically performed in the open.

5.5 No time for clemency

At a time when the clamour was for vengeance, pleas for moderation were ridiculed. When Governor General Canning declared that a gesture of leniency and a show of mercy would help in winning back the loyalty of the sepoys, he was mocked in the British press.

In one of the cartoons published in the pages of *Punch*, a British journal of comic satire, Canning is shown as a looming father figure, with his protective hand over the head of a sepoy who still holds an unsheathed sword in one hand and a dagger in the other, both dripping with blood (Fig.11.17) – an imagery that recurs in a number of British pictures of the time.

THE CLEMENCY OF CANNING.
Governor-General. "WELL, THEN, THEY SHAN'T BLOW HIM FROM NASTY GUNS; BUT HE MUST PROMISE TO BE A GOOD LITTLE SEPOY."

Fig. 11.17
"The Clemency of Canning", Punch, *24 October 1857*
The caption at the bottom of the cartoon reads: "Governor General: 'Well, then they shan't blow him from nasty guns; but he must promise to be a good little sepoy'."

5.6 Nationalist imageries

The national movement in the twentieth century drew its inspiration from the events of 1857. A whole world of nationalist imagination was woven around the revolt. It was celebrated as the First War of Independence in which all sections of the people of India came together to fight against imperial rule.

Art and literature, as much as the writing of history, have helped in keeping alive the memory of 1857. The leaders of the revolt were presented as heroic figures leading the country into battle, rousing the people to righteous indignation against oppressive imperial rule. Heroic poems were written about the valour of the queen who, with a sword in one hand and the reins of her horse in the other, fought for the freedom of her motherland. Rani of Jhansi was represented as a masculine figure chasing the enemy, slaying British soldiers and valiantly fighting till her last. Children in many parts of India grow up reading the lines of Subhadra Kumari Chauhan: *"Khoob lari mardani woh to Jhansi wali rani thi"* (Like a man she fought, she was the Rani of Jhansi). In popular prints Rani Lakshmi Bai is usually portrayed in battle armour, with a sword in hand and riding a horse – a symbol of the determination to resist injustice and alien rule.

Fig. 11.18
Films and posters have helped create the image of Rani Lakshmi Bai as a masculine warrior

The images indicate how the painters who produced them perceived those events, what they felt, and what they sought to convey. Through the paintings and cartoons we know about the public that looked at the paintings, appreciated or criticised the images, and bought copies and reproductions to put up in their homes.

These images did not only reflect the emotions and feelings of the times in which they were produced. They also shaped sensibilities. Fed by the images that circulated in Britain, the public sanctioned the most brutal forms of repression of the rebels. On the other hand, nationalist imageries of the revolt helped shape the nationalist imagination.

⊃ Discuss...

Examine the elements in each of the visuals in this section and discuss how they allow you to identify the perspective of the artist.

TIMELINE

1801	Subsidiary Alliance introduced by Wellesley in Awadh
1856	Nawab Wajid Ali Shah deposed; Awadh annexed
1856-57	Summary revenue settlements introduced in Awadh by the British
1857	
10 May	Mutiny starts in Meerut
11-12 May	Delhi garrisons revolt; Bahadur Shah accepts nominal leadership
20-27 May	Sepoys mutiny in Aligarh, Etawah, Mainpuri, Etah
30 May	Rising in Lucknow
May-June	Mutiny turns into a general revolt of the people
30 June	British suffer defeat in the battle of Chinhat
25 Sept	British forces under Havelock and Outram enter the Residency in Lucknow
July	Shah Mal killed in battle
1858	
June	Rani Jhansi killed in battle

ANSWER IN 100-150 WORDS

Fig. 11.19
Faces of rebels

1. Why did the mutinous sepoys in many places turn to erstwhile rulers to provide leadership to the revolt?

2. Discuss the evidence that indicates planning and coordination on the part of the rebels.

3. Discuss the extent to which religious beliefs shaped the events of 1857.

4. What were the measures taken to ensure unity among the rebels?

5. What steps did the British take to quell the uprising?

WRITE A SHORT ESSAY (250-300 WORDS) ON THE FOLLOWING:

6. Why was the revolt particularly widespread in Awadh? What prompted the peasants, *taluqdars* and zamindars to join the revolt?

7. What did the rebels want? To what extent did the vision of different social groups differ?

8. What do visual representations tell us about the revolt of 1857? How do historians analyse these representations?

9. Examine any two sources presented in the chapter, choosing one visual and one text, and discuss how these represent the point of view of the victor and the vanquished.

MAP WORK

10. On an outline map of India, mark Calcutta (Kolkata), Bombay (Mumbai) and Madras (Chennai), three major centres of British power in 1857. Refer to Maps 1 and 2 and plot the areas where the revolt was most widespread. How close or far were these areas from the colonial cities?

PROJECTS (CHOOSE ONE)

11. Read a biography of any one of the leaders of the revolt of 1857. Check the sources used by the biographer. Do these include government reports, newspaper accounts, stories in regional languages, visual material, anything else? Do all the sources say the same thing, or are there differences? Prepare a report on your findings.

12. See a film made on the revolt of 1857 and write about the way it represents the revolt. How does it depict the British, the rebels, and those who remained loyal to the British? What does it say about peasants, city dwellers, tribals, zamindars and *taluqdars*? What kind of a response does the film seek to evoke?

If you would like to know more, read:

Gautam Bhadra. 1987. 'Four Rebels of Eighteen-Fifty-Seven', *Subaltern Studies, IV*. Oxford University Press, Delhi.

Rudrangshu Mukherjee. 1984. *Awadh in Revolt, 1857-58*. Oxford University Press, Delhi.

Tapti Roy. 2006. *Raj of the Rani*. Penguin, New Delhi.

Eric Stokes. 1980. *Peasants and the Raj*. Oxford University Press, Delhi.

You could visit:
http://books.google.com
(for accounts of 1857 by British officials)

www.copsey-family.org/allenc/lakshmibai/links.html
(for letters of Rani Lakshmibai)

COLONIAL CITIES
URBANISATION, PLANNING AND ARCHITECTURE

In this chapter we will discuss the process of urbanisation in colonial India, explore the distinguishing characteristics of colonial cities and track social changes within them. We will look closely at developments in three big cities – Madras (Chennai), Calcutta (Kolkata) and Bombay (Mumbai).

All three were originally fishing and weaving villages. They became important centres of trade due to the economic activities of the English East India Company. Company agents settled in Madras in 1639 and in Calcutta in 1690. Bombay was given to the Company in 1661 by the English king, who had got it as part of his wife's dowry from the king of Portugal. The Company established trading and administrative offices in each of these settlements.

Fig. 12.1
South-east view of Fort St George, Madras, by Thomas and William Daniell,
based on a drawing by Daniell published in Oriental Scenery, *1798*
European ships carrying cargo dot the horizon. Country boats can be seen in the foreground.

By the middle of the nineteenth century these seltlements had become big cities from where the new rulers controlled the country. Institutions were set up to regulate economic activity and demonstrate the authority of the new rulers. Indians experienced political domination in new ways in these cities. The layouts of Madras, Bombay and Calcutta were quite different from older Indian towns, and the buildings that were built in these cities bore the marks of their colonial origin. What do buildings express and what can architecture convey? This is a question that students of history need to ask.

Remember that architecture helps in giving ideas a shape in stone, brick, wood or plaster. From the bungalow of the government officer, the palatial house of the rich merchant to the humble hut of the labourer, buildings reflect social relations and identities in many ways.

1. TOWNS AND CITIES IN PRE-COLONIAL TIMES

Before we explore the growth of cities in the colonial period, let us look at urban centres during the centuries preceding British rule.

1.1 What gave towns their character?

Towns were often defined in opposition to rural areas. They came to represent specific forms of economic activities and cultures. In the countryside people subsisted by cultivating land, foraging in the forest, or rearing animals. Towns by contrast were peopled with artisans, traders, administrators and rulers. Towns dominated over the rural population, thriving on the surplus and taxes derived from agriculture. Towns and cities were often fortified by walls which symbolised their separation from the countryside.

However, the separation between town and country was fluid. Peasants travelled long distances on pilgrimage, passing through towns; they also flocked to towns during times of famine. Besides, there was a reverse flow of humans and goods from towns to villages. When towns were attacked, people often sought shelter in the countryside. Traders and pedlars took goods from the towns to sell in the villages, extending markets and creating new patterns of consumption.

Source 1

Escaping to the countryside

This is how the famous poet Mirza Ghalib described what the people of Delhi did when the British forces occupied the city in 1857:

Smiting the enemy and driving him before them, the victors (i.e., the British) overran the city in all directions. All whom they found in the street they cut down ... For two to three days every road in the city, from the Kashmiri Gate to Chandni Chowk, was a battlefield. Three gates – the Ajmeri, the Turcoman and the Delhi – were still held by the rebels ... At the naked spectacle of this vengeful wrath and malevolent hatred the colour fled from men's faces, and a vast concourse of men and women ... took to precipitate flight through these three gates. Seeking the little villages and shrines outside the city, they drew breath to wait until such time as might favour their return.

During the sixteenth and seventeenth centuries the towns built by the Mughals were famous for their concentration of populations, their monumental buildings and their imperial grandeur and wealth. Agra, Delhi and Lahore were important centres of imperial administration and control. *Mansabdars* and *jagirdars* who were assigned territories in different parts of the empire usually maintained houses in these cities: residence in these centres of power was symbolic of the status and prestige of a noble.

The presence of the emperor and noblemen in these centres meant that a wide variety of services had to be provided. Artisans produced exclusive handicrafts for the households of nobles. Grain from the countryside was brought into urban markets for the town dwellers and the army. The treasury was also located in the imperial capital. Thus the revenues of the kingdom flowed into the capital regularly. The emperor lived in a fortified palace and the town was enclosed by a wall, with entry and exit being regulated by different gates. Within these towns were gardens, mosques, temples, tombs, colleges, bazaars and caravanserais. The focus of the town was oriented towards the palace and the principal mosque.

In the towns of South India such as Madurai and Kanchipuram the principal focus was the temple. These towns were also important commercial centres. Religious festivals often coincided with fairs, linking pilgrimage with trade. Generally, the ruler was the highest authority and the principal patron of religious institutions. The relationship that he had with other groups and classes determined their place in society and in the town.

Fig. 12.2
Shahjahanabad in 1857
The walls that surrounded the city were demolished after 1857. The Red Fort is on the river side.
At a distance on the ridge to the right, you can see the British settlements and the cantonment.

Medieval towns were places where everybody was expected to know their position in the social order dominated by the ruling elite. In North India, maintaining this order was the work of the imperial officer called the *kotwal* who oversaw the internal affairs and policing of the town.

1.2 Changes in the eighteenth century

All this started changing in the eighteenth century. With political and commercial realignments, old towns went into decline and new towns developed. The gradual erosion of Mughal power led to the demise of towns associated with their rule. The Mughal capitals, Delhi and Agra, lost their political authority. The growth of new regional powers was reflected in the increasing importance of regional capitals – Lucknow, Hyderabad, Seringapatam, Poona (present-day Pune), Nagpur, Baroda (present-day Vadodara) and Tanjore (present-day Thanjavur). Traders,, administrators, artisans and others migrated from the old Mughal centres to these new capitals in search of work and patronage. Continuous warfare between the new kingdoms meant that mercenaries too found ready employment there. Some local notables and officials associated with Mughal rule in North India also used this opportunity to create new urban settlements such as the *qasbah* and *ganj*. However, the effects of political decentralisation were uneven. In some places there was renewed economic activity, in other places war, plunder and political uncertainty led to economic decline.

Changes in the networks of trade were reflected in the history of urban centres. The European commercial Companies had set up base in different places early during the Mughal era: the Portuguese in Panaji in 1510, the Dutch in Masulipatnam in 1605, the British in Madras in 1639 and the French in Pondicherry (present-day Puducherry) in 1673. With the expansion of commercial activity, towns grew around these trading centres. By the end of the eighteenth century the land-based empires in Asia were replaced by the powerful

The *kotwal* of Delhi

Did you know that the first Prime Minister of India, Jawaharlal Nehru's grandfather, Ganga Dhar Nehru, was the *kotwal* of Delhi before the Revolt of 1857? Read Jawaharlal Nehru, *Autobiography,* for more details.

Qasbah is a small town in the countryside, often the seat of a local notable.
Ganj refers to a small fixed market.
Both *qasbah* and *ganj* dealt in cloth, fruit, vegetables and milk products. They provided for noble families and the army.

Fig. 12.3
A view of the city of Goa from the river, by J. Greig, 1812

Names of cities

Madras, Bombay and Calcutta were the Anglicised names of villages where the British first set up trading posts. They are now known as Chennai, Mumbai and Kolkata respectively.

➲ Discuss...

Which building, institution or place is the principal focus of the town, city or village in which you live? Explore its history. Find out when it was built, who built it, why it was built, what functions it served and whether these functions have changed.

sea-based European empires. Forces of international trade, mercantilism and capitalism now came to define the nature of society.

From the mid-eighteenth century, there was a new phase of change. Commercial centres such as Surat, Masulipatnam and Dhaka, which had grown in the seventeenth century, declined when trade shifted to other places. As the British gradually acquired political control after the Battle of Plassey in 1757, and the trade of the English East India Company expanded, colonial port cities such as Madras, Calcutta and Bombay rapidly emerged as the new economic capitals. They also became centres of colonial administration and political power. New buildings and institutions developed, and urban spaces were ordered in new ways. New occupations developed and people flocked to these colonial cities. By about 1800, they were the biggest cities in India in terms of population.

2. FINDING OUT ABOUT COLONIAL CITIES

2.1 Colonial records and urban history

Colonial rule was based on the production of enormous amounts of data. The British kept detailed records of their trading activities in order to regulate their commercial affairs. To keep track of life in the growing cities, they carried out regular surveys, gathered statistical data, and published various official reports.

From the early years, the colonial government was keen on mapping. It felt that good maps were necessary to understand the landscape and know the topography. This knowledge would allow better control over the region. When towns began to grow, maps were prepared not only to plan the development of these towns but also to develop commerce and consolidate power. The town maps give information regarding the location of hills, rivers and vegetation, all important for planning structures for defence purposes. They also show the location of *ghats*, density and quality of houses and alignment of roads, used to gauge commercial possibilities and plan strategies of taxation.

From the late nineteenth century the British tried to raise money for administering towns through the systematic annual collection of municipal taxes. To avoid conflict they handed over some responsibilities to elected Indian representatives. Institutions like the municipal corporation with some popular representation were meant to administer essential services such as water supply, sewerage, road building and public health. The activities of municipal corporations in turn generated a whole new set of records maintained in municipal record rooms.

The growth of cities was monitored through regular head-counts. By the mid-nineteenth century several local censuses had been carried out in different regions. The first all-India census was attempted in 1872. Thereafter, from 1881, decennial (conducted every ten years) censuses became a regular feature. This collection of data is an invaluable source for studying urbanisation in India.

When we look at these reports it appears that we have hard data to measure historical change. The endless pages of tables on disease and death, or the enumeration of people according their age, sex, caste and occupation, provide a vast mass of figures that creates an illusion of concreteness. Historians have, however, found that the figures can be misleading. Before we use these figures we need to understand who collected the data, and why and how they were gathered. We also need to know what was measured and what was not.

The census operation, for instance, was a means by which social data were converted into convenient statistics about the population. But this process was riddled with ambiguity. The census commissioners devised categories for classifying different sections of the population. This classification was often arbitrary and failed to capture the fluid and overlapping identities of people. How was a person who was both an artisan and a trader to be classified? How was a person who cultivated his land and carted produce to the town to be enumerated? Was he a cultivator or a trader?

Often people themselves refused to cooperate or gave evasive answers to the census officials.

Fig. 12.4
An old map of Bombay
The encircled area marked "castle" was part of the fortified settlement. The dotted areas show the seven islands that were gradually joined through projects of reclamation.

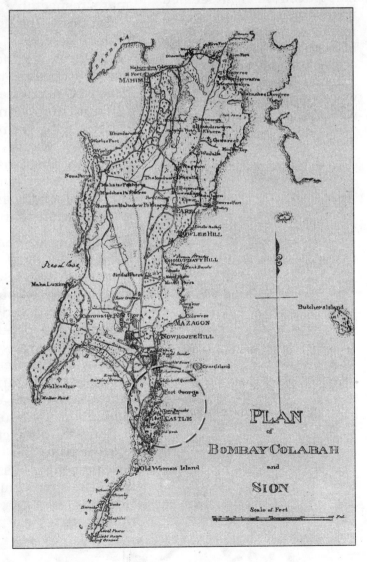

322

THEMES IN INDIAN HISTORY – PART III

What maps reveal and conceal

The development of survey methods, accurate scientific instruments and British imperial needs meant that maps were prepared with great care. The Survey of India was established in 1878. While the maps that were prepared give us a lot of information, they also reflect the bias of the British rulers. Large settlements of the poor in towns went unmarked on maps because they seemed unimportant to the rulers. As a result it was assumed that these blank spaces on the map were available for other development schemes. When these schemes were undertaken, the poor were evicted.

For a long while they were suspicious of census operations and believed that enquiries were being conducted to impose new taxes. Upper-caste people were also unwilling to give any information regarding the women of their household: women were supposed to remain secluded within the interior of the household and not subjected to public gaze or public enquiry.

Census officials also found that people were claiming identities that they associated with higher status. For instance there were people in towns who were hawkers and went selling small articles during some seasons, while in other seasons they earned their livelihood through manual labour. Such people often told the census enumerators that they were traders, not labourers, for they regarded trade as a more respectable activity.

Similarly, the figures of mortality and disease were difficult to collect, for all deaths were not registered, and illness was not always reported, nor treated by licensed doctors. How then could cases of illness or death be accurately calculated?

Thus historians have to use sources like the census with great caution, keeping in mind their possible biases, recalculating figures and understanding what the figures do not tell. However, census, survey maps and records of institutions like the municipality help us to study colonial cities in greater detail than is possible for pre-colonial cities.

2.2 Trends of change

A careful study of censuses reveals some fascinating trends. After 1800, urbanisation in India was sluggish. All through the nineteenth century up to the first two decades of the twentieth, the proportion of the urban population to the total population in India was extremely low and had remained stagnant. This is clear from Figure 12.5. In the forty years between 1900 and 1940 the urban population increased from about 10 per cent of the total population to about 13 per cent.

Beneath this picture of changelessness, there were significant variations in the patterns of urban development in different regions. The smaller towns had little opportunity to grow economically. Calcutta, Bombay and Madras on the other hand grew rapidly and soon became sprawling cities. In other words, the growth of these three cities as the new commercial and administrative centres was at the expense of other existing urban centres.

As the hub of the colonial economy, they functioned as collection depots for the export of Indian manufactures such as cotton textiles in the eighteenth and nineteenth centuries. After the Industrial Revolution in England, this trend was reversed and these cities instead became the entry point for British-manufactured goods and for the export of Indian raw materials. The nature of this economic activity sharply differentiated these colonial cities from India's traditional towns and urban settlements.

The introduction of railways in 1853 meant a change in the fortunes of towns. Economic activity gradually shifted away from traditional towns which were located along old routes and rivers. Every railway station became a collection depot for raw materials and a distribution point for imported goods. For instance, Mirzapur on the Ganges, which specialised in collecting cotton and cotton goods from the Deccan, declined when a railway link was made to Bombay (see Chapter 10, Figs. 10.18 and 10.19). With the expansion of the railway network, railway workshops and railway colonies were established. Railway towns like Jamalpur, Waltair and Bareilly developed.

Urbanisation in India 1891-1941	
Year	Percentage of urban population to total population
1891	9.4
1901	10.0
1911	9.4
1921	10.2
1931	11.1
1941	12.8

Fig. 12.5

⊃ Discuss...
Study either some statistical data or maps of a city. Check who collected the data and why they were collected. What are the possible biases in such collections? What kind of information is excluded? For the maps, find out why they were drawn and whether they are equally detailed for all parts of the city.

Fig. 12.6
The Borah Bazaar in the Fort area, Bombay, 1885
As Bombay grew, even the fort area became congested. Traders, shopkeepers and service groups flowed into the area, numerous bazaars were established, and lofty structures came up.
Worried by the congestion, the British made several attempts to push Indians out of the northern part of the Fort where the local communities had settled.

3. WHAT WERE THE NEW TOWNS LIKE?

3.1 Ports, forts and centres for services

Fig. 12.7
The Old Fort Ghat *in Calcutta, engraving by Thomas and William Daniell, 1787*
The Old Fort was on the water-front. The Company's goods were received here. The *ghat* continued to be used for bathing purposes by the local people.

By the eighteenth century Madras, Calcutta and Bombay had become important ports. The settlements that came up here were convenient points for collecting goods. The English East India Company built its factories (i.e., mercantile offices) there and because of competition among the European companies, fortified these settlements for protection. In Madras, Fort St George, in Calcutta Fort William and in Bombay the Fort marked out the areas of British settlement. Indian merchants, artisans and other workers who had economic dealings with European merchants lived outside these forts in settlements of their own. Thus, from the beginning there were separate quarters for Europeans and Indians, which came to be labelled in contemporary writings as the "White Town" and "Black Town" respectively. Once the British captured political power these racial distinctions became sharper.

From the mid-nineteenth century the expanding network of railways linked these cities to the rest of the country. As a result the hinterland – the countryside from where raw materials and labour were drawn – became more closely linked to these port cities. Since raw material was transported to these cities for export and there was plentiful cheap labour available, it was convenient to set up modern factories there. After the 1850s, cotton mills were set up by Indian merchants and entrepreneurs in Bombay, and European-owned jute mills were established on the outskirts of Calcutta. This was the beginning of modern industrial development in India.

Although Calcutta, Bombay and Madras supplied raw materials for industry in England, and had emerged because of modern economic forces like capitalism, their economies were not primarily based on factory production. The majority of the working population in these cities belonged to what economists classify as the tertiary sector. There were only two proper "industrial cities": Kanpur, specialising in leather, woollen and cotton textiles, and Jamshedpur, specialising in steel. India never became a modern industrialised country, since discriminatory colonial policies limited the levels of industrial development. Calcutta, Bombay and Madras grew into large cities, but this did not signify any dramatic economic growth for colonial India as a whole.

3.2 A new urban milieu

Colonial cities reflected the mercantile culture of the new rulers. Political power and patronage shifted from Indian rulers to the merchants of the East India Company. Indians who worked as interpreters, middlemen, traders and suppliers of goods also had an important place in these new cities. Economic activity near the river or the sea led to the development of docks and *ghats*. Along the shore were godowns, mercantile offices, insurance agencies for shipping, transport depots, banking establishments. Further inland were the chief administrative offices of the Company. The Writers' Building in Calcutta was one such office. Around the periphery of the Fort, European merchants and agents built palatial houses in European styles. Some built garden houses in the suburbs. Racially exclusive clubs, racecourses and theatres were also built for the ruling elite.

Ionic was one of the three orders (organisational systems) of Ancient Greek architecture, the other two being Doric, and Corinthian. One feature that distinguished each order was the style of the capital at the head of the columns. These forms were re-adapted in the Renaissance and Neo-classical forms of architecture.

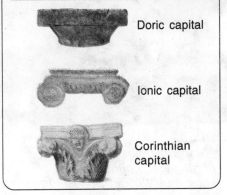

Doric capital

Ionic capital

Corinthian capital

Fig. 12.8
The Old Court House and Writers' Building, engraving by Thomas and William Daniell, 1786
The Court House on the right, with an open arcaded veranda and Ionic columns, was pulled down in 1792. Next to it is the Writers' Building where the East India Company servants in India (known as Writers) stayed on arrival in the country. Later this building became a government office.

Fig. 12.9
The New Buildings at Chourangee
(Chowringhee), engraving by
Thomas and William Daniell, 1787
Along the eastern side of the
Maidan private houses of the
British began coming up in the
late eighteenth century. Most were
in a Palladian style with pillared
verandas that were meant to
keep off the summer heat.

The rich Indian agents and middlemen built large
traditional courtyard houses in the Black Town in
the vicinity of the bazaars. They bought up large
tracts of land in the city as future investment. To
impress their English masters they threw lavish
parties during festivals. They also built temples to
establish their status in society. The labouring poor
provided a variety of services to their European
and Indian masters as cooks, palanquin bearers,
coachmen, guards, porters and construction and
dock workers. They lived in makeshift huts in
different parts of the city.

The nature of the colonial city changed further in
the mid-nineteenth century. After the Revolt of 1857
British attitudes in India were shaped by a constant
fear of rebellion. They felt that towns needed to be
better defended, and white people had to live in more
secure and segregated enclaves, away from the
threat of the "natives". Pasturelands and agricultural
fields around the older towns were cleared, and new
urban spaces called "Civil Lines" were set up. White
people began to live in the Civil Lines. Cantonments–
places where Indian troops under European
command were stationed – were also developed as
safe enclaves. These areas were separate from but
attached to the Indian towns. With broad streets,
bungalows set amidst large gardens, barracks,
parade ground and church, they were meant as a

Fig. 12.10
The Marble Palace, Calcutta
This is one of the most elaborate
structures built by an Indian family
belonging to the new urban elite.

Fig. 12.11
Chitpore Bazaar by Charles D'Oyly
Chitpore Bazaar was at the border of the Black Town and White Town in Calcutta. Notice the different types of houses here: the brick building of the wealthy landlord and the thatched huts of the poor. The temple in the picture, referred to by the British as the Black Pagoda, was built by a landlord, Govinda Ram Mitter, who lived here. Shaped by the language of race, even names were often coloured with blackness.

⊃ Look at Figures 12.8, 12.9 and 12.11. Notice the variety of activities on the streets. What do the activities tell us about the social life on the streets of Calcutta in the late eighteenth century?

safe haven for Europeans as well as a model of ordered urban life in contrast to the densely built-up Indian towns.

For the British, the "Black" areas came to symbolise not only chaos and anarchy, but also filth and disease. For a long while the British were interested primarily in the cleanliness and hygiene of the "White" areas. But as epidemics of cholera and plague spread, killing thousands, colonial officials felt the need for more stringent measures of sanitation and public health. They feared that disease would spread from the "Black" to the "White" areas. From the 1860s and 1870s, stringent administrative measures regarding sanitation were implemented and building activity in the Indian towns was regulated. Underground piped water supply and sewerage and drainage systems were also put in place around this time. Sanitary vigilance thus became another way of regulating Indian towns.

3.3 The first hill stations

As in the case of cantonments, hill stations were a distinctive feature of colonial urban development. The founding and settling of hill stations was initially connected with the needs of the British army. Simla (present-day Shimla) was founded during the course of the Gurkha War (1815-16); the Anglo-Maratha War of 1818 led to British interest in Mount Abu; and Darjeeling was wrested from the rulers of Sikkim in 1835. Hill stations became strategic places for billeting troops, guarding frontiers and launching campaigns against enemy rulers.

Fig. 12.12
A typical colonial house in Simla, an early-twentieth-century photograph
Most probably it was the residence of Sir John Marshall.

Fig. 12.13
A village near Manali, Himachal Pradesh
While the British introduced colonial architectural styles in the hill stations, the local population often continued to live as before.

The temperate and cool climate of the Indian hills was seen as an advantage, particularly since the British associated hot weather with epidemics. Cholera and malaria were particularly feared and attempts were made to protect the army from these diseases. The overwhelming presence of the army made these stations a new kind of cantonment in the hills. These hill stations were also developed as sanitariums, i.e., places where soldiers could be sent for rest and recovery from illnesses.

Because the hill stations approximated the cold climates of Europe, they became an attractive destination for the new rulers. It became a practice for viceroys to move to hill stations during the summer months. In 1864 the Viceroy John Lawrence officially moved his council to Simla, setting seal to the practice of shifting capitals during the hot season. Simla also became the official residence of the commander-in-chief of the Indian army.

In the hill stations the British and other Europeans sought to recreate settlements that were reminiscent of home. The buildings were deliberately built in the European style. Individual houses followed the pattern of detached villas and cottages set amidst gardens. The Anglican Church and educational institutions represented British ideals. Even recreation activities came to be shaped by British cultural traditions. Thus social calls, teas, picnics, fetes, races and visits to the theatre became common among colonial officials in the hill stations.

The introduction of the railways made hill stations more accessible to a wide range of people including Indians. Upper-and middle-class Indians such as maharajas, lawyers and merchants were drawn to these stations because they afforded them a close proximity to the ruling British elite.

Hill stations were important for the colonial economy. With the setting up of tea and coffee plantations in the adjoining areas, an influx of immigrant labour from the plains began. This meant that hill stations no longer remained exclusive racial enclaves for Europeans in India.

3.4 Social life in the new cities

For the Indian population, the new cities were bewildering places where life seemed always in a flux. There was a dramatic contrast between extreme wealth and poverty.

New transport facilities such as horse-drawn carriages and, subsequently, trams and buses meant that people could live at a distance from the city centre. Over time there was a gradual separation of the place of work from the place of residence. Travelling from home to office or the factory was a completely new kind of experience.

Also, though the sense of coherence and familiarity of the old towns was no longer there, the creation of public places – for example, public parks, theatres and, from the twentieth century, cinema halls – provided exciting new forms of entertainment and social interaction.

Within the cities new social groups were formed and the old identities of people were no longer important. All classes of people were migrating to the big cities. There was an increasing demand for clerks, teachers, lawyers, doctors, engineers and accountants. As a result the "middle classes" increased. They had access to new educational institutions such as schools, colleges and libraries. As educated people, they could put forward their opinions on society and government in newspapers, journals and public meetings. A new public sphere of debate and discussion emerged. Social customs, norms and practices came to be questioned.

Social changes did not happen with ease. Cities, for instance, offered new opportunities for women. Middle-class women sought to express themselves through the medium of journals, autobiographies and books. But many people resented these attempts to change traditional patriarchal norms. Conservatives feared that the education of women would turn the world upside down, and threaten the basis of the entire social order. Even reformers who supported women's education saw women primarily as mothers and wives, and wanted them to remain within the enclosed spaces of the household. Over time, women became more visible in public, as they entered new professions in the city as domestic

Fig. 12.14
Trams on a road in Calcutta

Amar Katha (My Story)

Binodini Dasi (1863-1941) was a pioneering figure in Bengali theatre in the late nineteenth and early twentieth centuries and worked closely with the dramatist and director Girish Chandra Ghosh (1844-1912). She was one of the prime movers behind the setting up of the Star Theatre (1883) in Calcutta which became a centre for famous productions. Between 1910 and 1913 she serialised her autobiography, *Amar Katha* (My Story). A remarkable personality, she exemplified the problem women faced in recasting their roles in society. She was a professional in the city, working in multiple spheres – as an actress, institution builder and author – but the patriarchal society of the time scorned her assertive public presence.

Fig. 12.15
A late-nineteenth-century Kalighat painting
Male anxiety about female power was often expressed through the figure of the woman as a charmer who transformed men into sheep. As women began to be educated and moved out of the seclusion of their homes, such images of women began to proliferate in popular prints.

and factory workers, teachers, and theatre and film actresses. But for a long time women who moved out of the household into public spaces remained the objects of social censure.

Another new class within the cities was the labouring poor or the working class. Paupers from rural areas flocked to the cities in the hope of employment. Some saw cities as places of opportunity; others were attracted by the allure of a different way of life, by the desire to see things they had never seen before. To minimise costs of living in the city, most male migrants left their families behind in their village homes. Life in the city was a struggle: jobs were uncertain, food was expensive, and places to stay were difficult to afford. Yet the poor often created a lively urban culture of their own. They were enthusiastic participants in religious festivals, *tamashas* (folk theatre) and *swangs* (satires) which often mocked the pretensions of their masters, Indian and European.

⊃ Discuss...
Which is the railway station closest to your residence? Find out when it was built and whether it was built to transport goods or people.
Ask older people what they know about the station. How often do you go to the station and why?

Source 2

Through the eyes of poor migrants

This is a *swang* that was popular amongst the inhabitants of *Jelepara* (Fishermen's quarter), Calcutta, in the early twentieth century:

Dil-me ek bhavna se Kalkatta-me aya

Kaisan kaisan maja ham hiya dekhne paya

Ari-samaj, Brahma-samaj, girja, mahjid

Ek lota-me milta – dudh, pani, sab chij

Chhota bara admi sab, bahar kar ke dat

Jhapat mar ke bolta hai, Angreji-me bat.

With anticipation in my heart I came to Calcutta

And what entertaining things I could see here!

The Arya Samaj, Brahmo Samaj, church and mosque –

In one vessel you get everything – milk, water and all

All men big and small show their teeth,

And with a flourish they speak in English.

4. SEGREGATION, TOWN PLANNING AND ARCHITECTURE

MADRAS, CALCUTTA AND BOMBAY

Madras, Calcutta and Bombay gradually developed into the biggest cities of colonial India. We have been examining some of the distinctive features of these cities in the preceding sections. Now we will look in detail at one characteristic for each city.

4.1 Settlement and segregation in Madras

The Company had first set up its trading activities in the well-established port of Surat on the west coast. Subsequently the search for textiles brought British merchants to the east coast. In 1639 they constructed a trading post in Madraspatam. This settlement was locally known as Chenapattanam. The Company had purchased the right of settlement from the local Telugu lords, the Nayaks of Kalahasti, who were eager to support trading activity in the region. Rivalry (1746-63) with the French East India Company led the British to fortify Madras and give their representatives increased political and administrative functions. With the defeat of the French in 1761, Madras became more secure and began to grow into an important commercial town. It was here that the superiority of the British and the subordinate position of the Indian merchants was most apparent.

Fort St George became the nucleus of the White Town where most of the Europeans lived. Walls and bastions made this a distinct enclave. Colour and religion determined who was allowed to live within the Fort. The Company did not permit any marriages with Indians. Other than the English, the Dutch and Portuguese were allowed to stay here because they were European and Christian. The administrative and judicial systems also favoured the white population. Despite being few in number the Europeans were the rulers and the development of Madras followed the needs and convenience of the minority whites in the town.

The Black Town developed outside the Fort. It was laid out in straight lines, a characteristic of colonial towns. It was, however, demolished in the mid-1700s and the area was cleared for a security zone around the Fort. A new Black Town developed further to the north. This housed weavers, artisans, middlemen and interpreters who played a vital role in the Company trade.

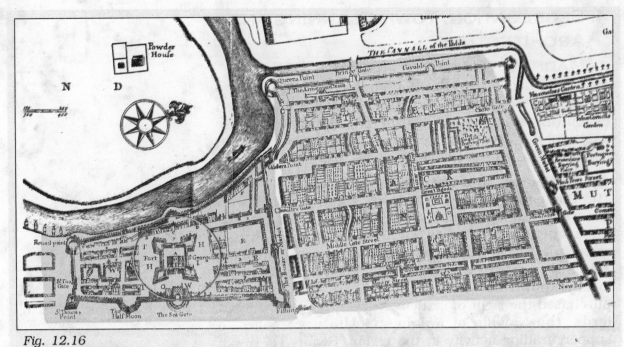

Fig. 12.16
A map of Madras
The White Town around Fort St George is on the left, and the Old Black Town is on the right. Fort St George is marked with a circle. Notice how the Black Town was laid out.

Fig. 12.17
Part of the Black Town, Madras, by Thomas and William Daniell, based on a drawing by Daniell published in Oriental Scenery, *1798*
The old Black Town was demolished to create the open space you see in this picture. Originally cleared as a line of fire, the open ground was later maintained as a green area. On the horizon you can see part of the new Black Town that came up at a distance from the Fort.

The new Black Town resembled traditional Indian towns, with living quarters built around its own temple and bazaar. On the narrow lanes that criss-crossed the township, there were distinct caste-specific neighbourhoods. Chintadripet was an area meant for weavers. Washermanpet was a colony of dyers and bleachers of cloth. Royapuram was a settlement for Christian boatmen who worked for the Company.

Madras developed by incorporating innumerable surrounding villages and by creating opportunities and spaces for a variety of communities. Several different communities came and settled in Madras, performing a range of economic functions. The *dubashes* were Indians who could speak two languages – the local language and English. They worked as agents and merchants, acting as intermediaries between Indian society and the British. They used their privileged position in government to acquire wealth. Their powerful position in society was established by their charitable works and patronage of temples in the Black Town.

Pet is a Tamil word meaning settlement, while *puram* is used for a village.

Initially jobs with the Company were monopolised by the Vellalars, a rural caste who took advantage of the new opportunities provided by British rule. With the spread of English education in the nineteenth century, Brahmins started competing for similar positions in the administration. Telugu Komatis were a powerful commercial group that controlled the grain trade in the city. Gujarati bankers had also been present since the eighteenth century. Paraiyars and Vanniyars formed the labouring poor. The Nawab of Arcot settled in nearby Triplicane which became the nucleus of a substantial Muslim settlement. Mylapore and Triplicane were earlier Hindu religious centres that supported a large group of Brahmins. San Thome with its cathedral was the centre for Roman Catholics. All these settlements became part of Madras city. Thus the incorporation of many villages made Madras a city of wide expanse and low density. This was noticed by European travellers and commented on by officials.

Fig. 12.18
A garden house on Poonamalee Road

Source 3

A rural city?

Read this excerpt on Madras from the *Imperial Gazetteer*, 1908:

> ... the better European residences are built in the midst of compounds which almost attain the dignity of parks; and rice-fields frequently wind in and out between these in almost rural fashion. Even in the most thickly peopled native quarters such as Black Town and Triplicane, there is little of the crowding found in many other towns ...

↻ Statements in reports often express the ideas of the reporter. What kind of an urban space is the reporter celebrating in the statement and what kind is he demeaning? Would you agree with these ideas?

As the British consolidated their power, resident Europeans began to move out of the Fort. Garden houses first started coming up along the two main arteries – Mount Road and Poonamalee Road – leading from the Fort to the cantonment. Wealthy Indians too started to live like the English. As a result many new suburbs were created from existing villages around the core of Madras. This was of course possible because the wealthy could afford transport. The poor settled in villages that were close to their place of work. The gradual urbanisation of Madras meant that the areas between these villages were brought within the city. As a result Madras had a semi-rural air about it.

4.2 Town planning in Calcutta

Modern town planning began in the colonial cities. This required preparation of a layout of the entire urban space and regulation of urban land use. Planning was usually inspired by a vision of what the city should look like, how it would be developed and the way in which spaces would be organised and ordered. The ideology of "development" that this vision reflected presumed exercise of state power over urban lives and urban spaces.

There were many reasons why the British took upon themselves the task of town planning from the early years of their rule in Bengal. One immediate reason was defence. In 1756, Sirajudaula, the Nawab of Bengal, attacked Calcutta and sacked the small fort which the British traders had built as their depot for goods. The English East India Company traders had been continuously questioning the sovereignty of the Nawab. They were reluctant to pay customs duties, and refused to comply with the terms on which they were expected to operate. So Sirajudaula wanted to assert his authority.

Subsequently, in 1757, when Sirajudaula was defeated in the Battle of Plassey, the East India Company decided to build a new fort, one that could not be easily attacked. Calcutta had grown from three villages called Sutanati, Kolkata and Govindapur. The Company cleared a site in the southernmost village of Govindapur and the traders and weavers living there were asked to move out. Around the new Fort William they left a vast open space which came to be locally known as the Maidan or *garer-math*.

This was done so that there would be no obstructions to a straight line of fire from the Fort against an advancing enemy army. Once the British became more confident about their permanent presence in Calcutta, they started moving out of the Fort and building residences along the periphery of the Maidan. That was how the English settlement in Calcutta gradually started taking shape. The vast open space around the Fort (which still exists) became a landmark, Calcutta's first significant town planning measure.

The history of town planning in Calcutta of course did not end with the building of Fort William and the Maidan. In 1798, Lord Wellesley became the Governor General. He built a massive palace, Government House, for himself in Calcutta, a building that was expected to convey the authority of the British. He became concerned about the condition of the Indian part of the city – the crowding, the excessive vegetation, the dirty tanks, the smells and poor drainage. These conditions worried the British because they believed at the time that poisonous gases from marshlands and pools of stagnant water were the cause of most diseases. The tropical climate itself was seen as unhealthy

The line of fire

Interestingly, the pattern devised for Calcutta was replicated in many other towns. During the Revolt of 1857 many towns became rebel strongholds. After their victory the British proceeded to make these places safe for themselves. In Delhi for instance they took over the Red Fort and stationed an army there. Then they destroyed buildings close to the Fort creating a substantial empty space between the Indian neighbourhoods and the Fort. The logic was the same as in Calcutta a hundred years ago: a direct line of fire was considered essential, just in case the town rose up against *firangi raj* once again.

Fig. 12.19
Government House, Calcutta, by Charles D'Oyly, 1848
The residence of the Governor General, the Government House, built by Wellesley, was meant to symbolise the grandeur of the Raj.

Fig. 12.20
A bazaar leading to Chitpore Road in Calcutta
For local communities in the towns, the bazaar was a place of both commercial and social exchange. Europeans were fascinated by the bazaar but also saw it as an overcrowded and dirty place.

Source 4

"For the regulation of nuisances of every description"

By the early nineteenth century the British felt that permanent and public rules had to be formulated for regulating all aspects of social life. Even the construction of private buildings and public roads ought to conform to standardised rules that were clearly codified. In his Minute on Calcutta (1803) Wellesley wrote:

It is a primary duty of Government to provide for the health, safety and convenience of the inhabitants of this great town, by establishing a comprehensive system for the improvement of roads, streets, public drains, and water courses, and by fixing permanent rules for the construction and distribution of the houses and public edifices, and for the regulation of nuisances of every description.

and enervating. Creating open places in the city was one way of making the city healthier. Wellesley wrote a Minute (an administrative order) in 1803 on the need for town planning, and set up various committees for the purpose. Many bazaars, *ghats*, burial grounds, and tanneries were cleared or removed. From then on the notion of "public health" became an idea that was proclaimed in projects of town clearance and town planning.

After Wellesley's departure the work of town planning was carried on by the Lottery Committee (1817) with the help of the government. The Lottery Committee was so named because funds for town improvement were raised through public lotteries. In other words, in the early decades of the nineteenth century raising funds for the city was still thought to be the responsibility of public-minded citizens and not exclusively that of the government. The Lottery Committee commissioned a new map of the city so as to get a comprehensive picture of Calcutta. Among the Committee's major activities was road building in the Indian part of the city and clearing the river bank of "encroachments". In its drive to make the Indian areas of Calcutta cleaner, the committee removed many huts and displaced the labouring poor, who were now pushed to the outskirts of Calcutta.

The threat of epidemics gave a further impetus to town planning in the next few decades. Cholera started spreading from 1817 and in 1896 plague made its appearance. The cause of these diseases had not yet been established firmly by medical science. The government proceeded on the basis of the accepted theory of the time: that there was a direct correlation between living conditions and the spread of disease. Such views were supported by prominent Indian merchants in the city, such as Dwarkanath Tagore and Rustomjee Cowasjee, who felt that Calcutta needed to be made more healthy. Densely built-up areas were seen as insanitary since they obstructed direct sunlight and circulation of air. That was why working people's huts or "*bustis*" became the target of demolition. The poor in the city – workers, hawkers, artisans, porters and the unemployed – were once again forced to move to distant parts of the city. Frequent fires also led to stricter building regulations – for instance, thatched huts were banned in 1836 and tiled roofs made mandatory.

By the late nineteenth century, official intervention in the city became more stringent. Gone were the days when town planning was seen as a task to be shared by inhabitants and the government. Instead, the government took over all the initiatives for town planning including funding. This opportunity was used to clear more huts and develop the British portions of the town at the expense of other areas. The existing racial divide of the "White Town" and "Black Town" was reinforced by the new divide of "healthy" and "unhealthy". Indian representatives in the municipality protested against this unfair bias towards the development of the European parts of the town. Public protests against these government policies strengthened the feeling of anti-colonialism and nationalism among Indians.

> ⊃ How does Wellesley define the duty of the government? Read this section and discuss what impact these ideas, if implemented, would have had on the Indians living in the city.

Busti (in Bengali and Hindi) originally meant neighbourhood or settlement. However, the British narrowed the sense of the word to mean makeshift huts built by the poor. In the late nineteenth century "*bustis*" and insanitary slums became synonymous in British records.

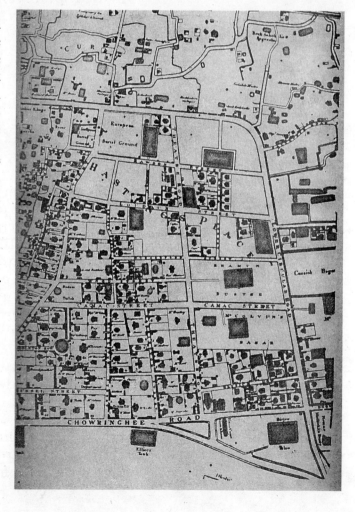

Fig. 12.21
A part of the European town in Calcutta after the Lottery Committee improvements, from the plan by J.A. Schalch (1825)
You can see the European houses with compounds.

Fig. 12.22
A busti *in Calcutta*

With the growth of their empire, the British became increasingly inclined to make cities like Calcutta, Bombay and Madras into impressive imperial capitals. It was as if the grandeur of the cities had to reflect the authority of imperial power. Town planning had to represent everything that the British claimed to stand for: rational ordering, meticulous execution, and Western aesthetic ideals. Cities had to be cleaned and ordered, planned and beautified.

4.3 Architecture in Bombay

If one way of realising this imperial vision was through town planning, the other was through embellishing cities with monumental buildings. Buildings in cities could include forts, government offices, educational institutions, religious structures, commemorative towers, commercial depots, or even docks and bridges. Although primarily serving functional needs like defence, administration and commerce these were rarely simple structures. They were often meant to represent ideas such as imperial power, nationalism and religious glory. Let us see how this is exemplified in the case of Bombay.

Bombay was initially seven islands. As the population grew, the islands were joined to create more space and they gradually fused into one big city. Bombay was the commercial capital of colonial India. As the premier port on the western coast it was the centre of international trade. By the end of the nineteenth century, half the imports and exports of India passed through Bombay. One important item of this trade was opium that the East India Company exported to China. Indian merchants and middlemen supplied and participated in this trade and they helped integrate Bombay's economy directly to Malwa, Rajasthan and Sind where opium was grown. This collaboration with the Company was profitable and led to the growth of an Indian capitalist class. Bombay's capitalists came from diverse communities such as Parsi, Marwari, Konkani Muslim, Gujarati Bania, Bohra, Jew and Armenian.

As you have read (Chapter 10), when the American Civil War started in 1861 cotton from the American South stopped coming into the international market. This led to an upsurge of demand for Indian cotton, grown primarily in the Deccan. Once again Indian merchants and middlemen found an opportunity for earning huge profits. In 1869 the Suez Canal was opened and this further strengthened Bombay's links with the world economy. The Bombay government and Indian merchants used this opportunity to declare Bombay *Urbs Prima in Indis*, a Latin phrase meaning the most important city of India. By the late nineteenth century Indian merchants in Bombay were investing their wealth in new ventures such as cotton mills. They also patronised building activity in the city.

As Bombay's economy grew, from the mid-nineteenth century there was a need to expand railways and shipping and develop the administrative structure. Many new buildings were constructed at this time. These buildings reflected the culture and confidence of the rulers. The architectural style was usually European. This importation of European styles reflected the imperial vision in several ways. First, it expressed the British desire to create a familiar landscape in an alien country, and thus to feel at home in the colony. Second, the British felt that European styles would best symbolise their superiority, authority and power. Third, they thought that buildings that looked European would mark out the difference and distance between the colonial masters and their Indian subjects.

Initially, these buildings were at odds with the traditional Indian buildings. Gradually, Indians too got used to European architecture and made it their own. The British in turn adapted some Indian styles to suit their needs. One example is the bungalow which was used by government officers in Bombay and all over India. The name bungalow was derived from *bangla*, a traditional thatched Bengali hut. The colonial bungalow was set on extensive grounds which ensured privacy and marked a distance from the Indian world around. The traditional pitched roof and surrounding veranda kept the bungalow cool in the summer months. The compound had separate quarters for a retinue of domestic servants. The

Fig. 12.23
A bungalow in Bombay, nineteenth century

Fig. 12.24
The Town Hall in Bombay, which now houses the Asiatic Society of Bombay

Pitched roof is a term used by architects to describe a sloping roof. By the early twentieth century pitched roofs became less common in bungalows, although the general plan remained the same.

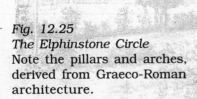

Fig. 12.23
A bungalow in Bombay, nineteenth century

Fig. 12.25
The Elphinstone Circle
Note the pillars and arches, derived from Graeco-Roman architecture.

bungalows in the Civil Lines thus became a racially exclusive enclave in which the ruling classes could live self-sufficient lives without daily social contact with Indians.

For pubic buildings three broad architectural styles were used. Two of these were direct imports from fashions prevalent in England. The first was called neo-classical or the new classical. Its characteristics included construction of geometrical structures fronted with lofty pillars It was derived from a style that was originally typical of buildings in ancient Rome, and was subsequently revived, re-adapted and made popular during the European Renaissance. It was considered particularly appropriate for the British Empire in India. The British imagined that a style that embodied the grandeur of imperial Rome could now be made to express the glory of imperial India. The Mediterranean origins of this architecture were also thought to be suitable for tropical weather. The Town Hall in Bombay (Fig. 12.24) was built in this style in 1833. Another group of commercial buildings, built during the cotton boom of the 1860s, was the Elphinstone Circle. Subsequently named Horniman Circle after an English editor who courageously supported Indian nationalists, this building was inspired from models in Italy. It made innovative use of covered arcades at ground level to shield the shopper and pedestrian from the fierce sun and rain of Bombay.

Another style that was extensively used was the neo-Gothic, characterised by high-pitched roofs, pointed arches and detailed decoration. The Gothic style had its roots in buildings, especially churches, built in northern Europe during the medieval period. The neo-Gothic or new Gothic style was revived in the mid-nineteenth century in England. This was the time when the government in Bombay was building its infrastructure and this style was adapted for Bombay. An impressive group of buildings facing the seafront including the Secretariat, University of Bombay and High Court were all built in this style.

Indians gave money for some of these buildings. The University Hall was made with money donated by Sir Cowasjee Jehangir Readymoney, a rich Parsi merchant. The University Library clock tower was similarly funded by the banker Premchand Roychand and was named after his mother as Rajabai Tower. Indian merchants were happy to adopt the neo-Gothic style since they believed that building styles, like many ideas brought in by the English, were progressive and would help make Bombay into a modern city.

However, the most spectacular example of the neo-Gothic style is the Victoria Terminus, the station and headquarters of the Great Indian Peninsular Railway Company. The British

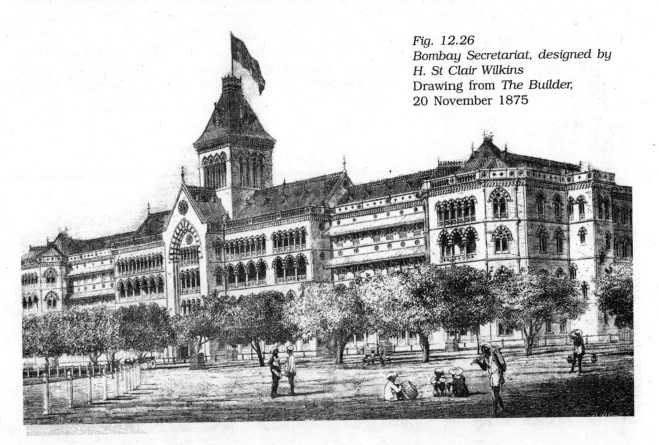

Fig. 12.26
Bombay Secretariat, designed by H. St Clair Wilkins
Drawing from *The Builder*, 20 November 1875

Fig. 12.27
*Victoria Terminus Railway
Station, designed by
F.W. Stevens*

Fig. 12.28
Madras law courts
While Bombay remained the
main centre of Gothic revival,
Indo-Saracenic flourished in
Madras. The design of the law
courts combined Pathan
elements with Gothic ones.

invested a lot in the design and construction of railway stations in cities, since they were proud of having successfully built an all-India railway network. As a group these buildings dominated the central Bombay skyline and their uniform neo-Gothic style gave a distinctive character to the city.

Towards the beginning of the twentieth century a new hybrid architectural style developed which combined the Indian with the European. This was called Indo-Saracenic. "Indo" was shorthand for Hindu and "Saracen" was a term Europeans used to designate Muslim. The inspiration for this style was medieval buildings in India with their domes, *chhatris*, *jalis*, arches. By integrating Indian and European styles in public architecture the British wanted to prove that they were legitimate rulers of India. The Gateway of India, built in the traditional Gujarati style to welcome King George V and Queen Mary to India in 1911, is the most famous example of this style. The industrialist Jamsetji Tata built the Taj Mahal Hotel in a similar style. Besides being a symbol of Indian enterprise, this building became

a challenge to the racially exclusive clubs and hotels maintained by the British.

In the more "Indian" localities of Bombay traditional styles of decoration and building predominated. The lack of space in the city and crowding led to a type of building unique to Bombay, the *chawl*, the multi-storeyed single-room apartments with long open corridors built around a courtyard. Such buildings which housed many families sharing common spaces helped in the growth of neighbourhood identity and solidarity.

5. WHAT BUILDINGS AND ARCHITECTURAL STYLES TELL US

Architecture reflects the aesthetic ideals prevalent at a time, and variations within those ideals. But, as we have seen, buildings also express the vision of those who build them. Rulers everywhere seek to express their power through buildings. So by looking at the architecture of a particular time, we can understand how power was conceived of and how it was expressed through structures and their attributes – bricks and stones, pillars and arches, soaring domes or vaulted roofs.

Fig. 12.29
The Municipal Corporation Building, Bombay, designed by F. W. Stevens in 1888
Notice the fusion of Oriental and Gothic designs.

Fig. 12.30
A Bombay chawl

Architectural styles do not only reflect prevalent tastes. They mould tastes, popularise styles and shape the contours of culture. As we have seen, many Indians came to regard European styles of architecture as symbols of modernity and civilisation, and began adopting these styles. But not all Indians thought alike: many rejected European ideals and tried to retain indigenous styles; others accepted certain elements from the West that they saw as modern and combined these with elements drawn from local traditions. From the late nineteenth century we see efforts to define regional and national tastes that were different from the colonial ideal. Styles thus changed and developed through wider processes of cultural conflict. By looking at architecture therefore we can also understand the variety of forms in which cultural conflicts unfolded and political conflicts – between the imperial and the national, the national and the regional/local – were played out.

⊃ Discuss...
Choose a historical building that you admire. List its architectural attributes and find out about its style and why that particular style was adopted.

TIMELINE

1500-1700	European trading companies establish bases in India: the Portuguese in Panaji in 1510; the Dutch in Masulipatnam, 1605; the British in Madras in 1639, in Bombay in 1661, and in Calcutta in 1690; the French in Pondicherry in 1673
1757	Decisive victory of the British in the Battle of Plassey; the British become rulers of Bengal
1773	Supreme Court set up in Calcutta by the East India Company
1803	Lord Wellesley's Minute on Calcutta town improvement
1818	British takeover of the Deccan; Bombay becomes the capital of the new province
1853	Railway from Bombay to Thane
1857	First spinning and weaving mill in Bombay
1857	Universities in Bombay, Madras and Calcutta
1870s	Beginning of elected representatives in municipalities
1881	Madras harbour completed
1896	First screening of a film at Watson's Hotel, Bombay
1896	Plague starts spreading to major cities
1911	Transfer of capital from Calcutta to Delhi

ANSWER IN 100-150 WORDS

1. To what extent are census data useful in reconstructing patterns of urbanisation in the colonial context?

2. What do the terms "White" and "Black" Town signify?

3. How did prominent Indian merchants establish themselves in the colonial city?

4. Examine how concerns of defence and health gave shape to Calcutta.

5. What are the different colonial architectural styles which can be seen in Bombay city?

WRITE A SHORT ESSAY (250-300 WORDS) ON THE FOLLOWING:

6. How were urban centres transformed during the eighteenth century?

7. What were the new kinds of public places that emerged in the colonial city? What functions did they serve?

8. What were the concerns that influenced town planning in the nineteenth century?

9. To what extent were social relations transformed in the new cities?

MAP WORK

10. On an outline map of India, trace the major rivers and hill ranges. Plot ten cities mentioned in the chapter, including Bombay, Calcutta and Madras, and prepare a brief note on why the importance of any two cities that you have marked (one colonial and one pre-colonial) changed in the nineteenth century.

PROJECT (CHOOSE ONE)

11. You have been reading about big colonial cities. Choose any small town with a long history. It could be a temple town, market town, administrative centre, a pilgrimage centre or a combination of these. Find out how the town was established, when it developed, and how its history changed during modern times.

12. Choose five different types of buildings in your town or village. For each of these, find out when it was built, how it was planned, how resources were obtained for its construction, and how long it took to build it. What do the architectural features of the buildings express?

If you would like to know more, read:

Sabyasachi Bhattacharya.1990. *Adhunik Bharat Ka Aarthik Itihas.* Rajkamal Prakashan, Delhi.

Norma Evenson. 1989. *The Indian Metropolis: A View Toward the West.* Oxford University Press, Delhi.

Narayani Gupta. 1981. *Delhi between Two Empires 1803-1931.* Oxford University Press, Delhi.

Gavin Hambly and Burton Stein. "Towns and Cities", in Tapan Raychaudhuri and Irfan Habib edited, *The Cambridge Economic History of India,* (Volume I), 1984. Orient Longman and Cambridge University Press, Delhi.

Anthony King. 1976. *Colonial Urban Development: Culture, Social Power and Environment* Routledge and Kegan Paul, London.

Thomas R. Metcalf. 1989. *An Imperial Vision: Indian Architecture and Britain's Raj* Faber and Faber, London.

Lewis Mumford. 1961. *The City in History: Its Origins, Its Transformations and Its Prospects.* Secker and Warburg, London.

THEME THIRTEEN

MAHATMA GANDHI AND THE NATIONALIST MOVEMENT
CIVIL DISOBEDIENCE AND BEYOND

In the history of nationalism a single individual is often identified with the making of a nation. Thus, for example, we associate Garibaldi with the making of Italy, George Washington with the American War of Independence, and Ho Chi Minh with the struggle to free Vietnam from colonial rule. In the same manner, Mahatma Gandhi has been regarded as the 'Father' of the Indian nation.

In so far as Gandhiji was the most influential and revered of all the leaders who participated in the freedom struggle, that characterisation is not misplaced. However, like Washington or Ho Chi-Minh, Mahatma Gandhi's political career was shaped and constrained by the society in which he lived. For individuals, even great ones, are made by history even as they make history.

This chapter analyses Gandhiji's activities in India during the crucial period 1915-1948. It explores his interactions with different sections of the Indian society and the popular struggles that he inspired and led. It introduces the student to the different kinds of sources that historians use in reconstructing the career of a leader and of the social movements that he was associated with.

Fig. 13.1
People gather on the banks of the Sabarmati River to hear Mahatma Gandhi speak before starting out on the Salt March in 1930

1. A LEADER ANNOUNCES HIMSELF

In January 1915, Mohandas Karamchand Gandhi returned to his homeland after two decades of residence abroad. These years had been spent for the most part in South Africa, where he went as a lawyer, and in time became a leader of the Indian community in that territory. As the historian Chandran Devanesan has remarked, South Africa was "the making of the Mahatma". It was in South Africa that Mahatma Gandhi first forged the distinctive techniques of non-violent protest known as satyagraha, first promoted harmony between religions, and first alerted upper-caste Indians to their discriminatory treatment of low castes and women.

The India that Mahatma Gandhi came back to in 1915 was rather different from the one that he had left in 1893. Although still a colony of the British, it was far more active in a political sense. The Indian National Congress now had branches in most major cities and towns. Through the Swadeshi movement of 1905-07 it had greatly broadened its appeal among the middle classes. That movement had thrown up some towering leaders – among them Bal Gangadhar Tilak of Maharashtra, Bipin Chandra Pal of Bengal, and Lala Lajpat Rai of Punjab. The three were known as "Lal, Bal and Pal", the alliteration conveying the all-India character of their struggle, since their native provinces were very distant from one another. Where these leaders advocated militant opposition to colonial rule, there was a group of "Moderates" who preferred a more gradual and persuasive approach. Among these Moderates was Gandhiji's acknowledged political mentor, Gopal Krishna Gokhale, as well as Mohammad Ali Jinnah, who, like Gandhiji, was a lawyer of Gujarati extraction trained in London.

On Gokhale's advice, Gandhiji spent a year travelling around British India, getting to know the land and its peoples. His first major public appearance was at the opening of the Banaras Hindu University (BHU) in February 1916. Among the invitees to

Fig. 13.2
Mahatma Gandhi in Johannesburg, South Africa, February 1908

this event were the princes and philanthropists whose donations had contributed to the founding of the BHU. Also present were important leaders of the Congress, such as Annie Besant. Compared to these dignitaries, Gandhiji was relatively unknown. He had been invited on account of his work in South Africa, rather than his status within India.

When his turn came to speak, Gandhiji charged the Indian elite with a lack of concern for the labouring poor. The opening of the BHU, he said, was "certainly a most gorgeous show". But he worried about the contrast between the "richly bedecked noblemen" present and "millions of the poor" Indians who were absent. Gandhiji told the privileged invitees that "there is no salvation for India unless you strip yourself of this jewellery and hold it in trust for your countrymen in India". "There can be no spirit of self-government about us," he went on, "if we take away or allow others to take away from the peasants almost the whole of the results of their labour. Our salvation can only come through the farmer. Neither the lawyers, nor the doctors, nor the rich landlords are going to secure it."

The opening of the BHU was an occasion for celebration, marking as it did the opening of a nationalist university, sustained by Indian money and Indian initiative. But rather than adopt a tone of self-congratulation, Gandhiji chose instead to remind those present of the peasants and workers who constituted a majority of the Indian population, yet were unrepresented in the audience.

Gandhiji's speech at Banaras in February 1916 was, at one level, merely a statement of fact – namely, that Indian nationalism was an elite phenomenon, a creation of lawyers and doctors and landlords. But, at another level, it was also a statement of intent – the first public announcement of Gandhiji's own desire to make Indian nationalism more properly

Fig. 13.3
Mahatma Gandhi in Karachi,
March 1916

representative of the Indian people as a whole. In the last month of that year, Gandhiji was presented with an opportunity to put his precepts into practice. At the annual Congress, held in Lucknow in December 1916, he was approached by a peasant from Champaran in Bihar, who told him about the harsh treatment of peasants by British indigo planters.

2. The Making and Unmaking of Non-cooperation

Mahatma Gandhi was to spend much of 1917 in Champaran, seeking to obtain for the peasants security of tenure as well as the freedom to cultivate the crops of their choice. The following year, 1918, Gandhiji was involved in two campaigns in his home state of Gujarat. First, he intervened in a labour dispute in Ahmedabad, demanding better working conditions for the textile mill workers. Then he joined peasants in Kheda in asking the state for the remission of taxes following the failure of their harvest.

These initiatives in Champaran, Ahmedabad and Kheda marked Gandhiji out as a nationalist with a deep sympathy for the poor. At the same time, these were all localised struggles. Then, in 1919, the colonial rulers delivered into Gandhiji's lap an issue from which he could construct a much wider movement. During the Great War of 1914-18, the British had instituted censorship of the press and permitted detention without trial. Now, on the recommendation of a committee chaired by Sir Sidney Rowlatt, these tough measures were continued. In response, Gandhiji called for a countrywide campaign against the "Rowlatt Act". In towns across North and West India, life came to a standstill, as shops shut down and schools closed in response to the *bandh* call. The protests were particularly intense in the Punjab, where many men had served on the British side in the War – expecting to be rewarded for their service. Instead they were given the Rowlatt Act. Gandhiji was detained while proceeding to the Punjab, even as prominent local Congressmen were arrested. The situation in the province grew progressively more tense, reaching a bloody climax in Amritsar in April 1919, when a British Brigadier ordered his troops to open fire on a nationalist meeting. More

⊃ Discuss...
Find out more about the national movement in India before 1915 and see whether Mahatma Gandhi's comments are justified.

than four hundred people were killed in what is known as the Jallianwala Bagh massacre.

It was the Rowlatt satyagraha that made Gandhiji a truly *national* leader. Emboldened by its success, Gandhiji called for a campaign of "non-cooperation" with British rule. Indians who wished colonialism to end were asked to stop attending schools, colleges and law courts, and not pay taxes. In sum, they were asked to adhere to a "renunciation of (all) voluntary association with the (British) Government". If non-cooperation was effectively carried out, said Gandhiji, India would win swaraj within a year. To further broaden the struggle he had joined hands with the Khilafat Movement that sought to restore the Caliphate, a symbol of Pan-Islamism which had recently been abolished by the Turkish ruler Kemal Attaturk.

2.1 Knitting a popular movement

Gandhiji hoped that by coupling non-cooperation with Khilafat, India's two major religious communities, Hindus and Muslims, could collectively bring an end to colonial rule. These movements certainly unleashed a surge of popular action that was altogether unprecedented in colonial India.

Students stopped going to schools and colleges run by the government. Lawyers refused to attend court. The working class went on strike in many towns and cities: according to official figures, there were 396 strikes in 1921, involving 600,000 workers and a loss of seven million workdays. The countryside was seething with discontent too. Hill tribes in northern Andhra violated the forest laws. Farmers in Awadh did not pay taxes. Peasants in Kumaun refused to carry loads for colonial officials. These protest movements were sometimes carried out in defiance of the local nationalist leadership. Peasants, workers, and others interpreted and acted upon the call to "non-cooperate" with colonial rule in ways that best suited their interests, rather than conform to the dictates laid down from above.

"Non-cooperation," wrote Mahatma Gandhi's American biographer Louis Fischer, "became the name of an epoch in the life of India and of Gandhiji. Non-cooperation was negative enough to be peaceful but positive enough to be effective. It entailed denial, renunciation, and self-discipline. It was training for

What was the Khilafat Movement?

The Khilafat Movement, (1919-1920) was a movement of Indian Muslims, led by Muhammad Ali and Shaukat Ali, that demanded the following: The Turkish Sultan or Khalifa must retain control over the Muslim sacred places in the erstwhile Ottoman empire; the *jazirat-ul-Arab* (Arabia, Syria, Iraq, Palestine) must remain under Muslim sovereignty; and the Khalifa must be left with sufficient territory to enable him to defend the Islamic faith. The Congress supported the movement and Mahatma Gandhi sought to conjoin it to the Non-cooperation Movement.

self-rule." As a consequence of the Non-Cooperation Movement the British Raj was shaken to its foundations for the first time since the Revolt of 1857. Then, in February 1922, a group of peasants attacked and torched a police station in the hamlet of Chauri Chaura, in the United Provinces (now, Uttar Pradesh and Uttaranchal). Several constables perished in the conflagration. This act of violence prompted Gandhiji to call off the movement altogether. "No provocation," he insisted, "can possibly justify (the) brutal murder of men who had been rendered defenceless and who had virtually thrown themselves on the mercy of the mob."

Fig. 13.4
Non-cooperation Movement, July 1922
Foreign cloth being collected to be burnt in bonfires.

During the Non-Cooperation Movement thousands of Indians were put in jail. Gandhiji himself was arrested in March 1922, and charged with sedition. The judge who presided over his trial, Justice C.N. Broomfield, made a remarkable speech while pronouncing his sentence. "It would be impossible to ignore the fact," remarked the judge, "that you are in a different category from any person I have ever tried or am likely to try. It would be impossible to ignore the fact that, in the eyes of millions of your countrymen, you are a great patriot and a leader. Even those who differ from you in politics look upon you as a man of high ideals and of even saintly life." Since Gandhiji had violated the law it was obligatory for the Bench to sentence him to six years' imprisonment, but, said Judge Broomfield, "If the course of events in India should make it possible for the Government to reduce the period and release you, no one will be better pleased than I".

2.2 A people's leader

By 1922, Gandhiji had transformed Indian nationalism, thereby redeeming the promise he made in his BHU speech of February 1916. It was no longer a movement of professionals and intellectuals; now, hundreds of thousands of peasants, workers and artisans also participated in it. Many of them venerated Gandhiji, referring to him as their

"Mahatma". They appreciated the fact that he dressed like them, lived like them, and spoke their language. Unlike other leaders he did not stand apart from the common folk, but empathised and even identified with them.

This identification was strikingly reflected in his dress: while other nationalist leaders dressed formally, wearing a Western suit or an Indian *bandgala*, Gandhiji went among the people in a simple *dhoti* or loincloth. Meanwhile, he spent part of each day working on the *charkha* (spinning wheel), and encouraged other nationalists to do likewise. The act of spinning allowed Gandhiji to break the boundaries that prevailed within the traditional caste system, between mental labour and manual labour.

In a fascinating study, the historian Shahid Amin has traced the image of Mahatma Gandhi among the peasants of eastern Uttar Pradesh, as conveyed by reports and rumours in the local press. When he travelled through the region in February 1921, Gandhiji was received by adoring crowds everywhere.

Fig. 13.5
Mahatma Gandhi with the charkha *has become the most abiding image of Indian nationalism.*
In 1921, during a tour of South India, Gandhiji shaved his head and began wearing a loincloth in order to identify with the poor. His new appearance also came to symbolise asceticism and abstinence – qualities he celebrated in opposition to the consumerist culture of the modern world.

Source 1

Charkha

Mahatma Gandhi was profoundly critical of the modern age in which machines enslaved humans and displaced labour. He saw the *charkha* as a symbol of a human society that would not glorify machines and technology. The spinning wheel, moreover, could provide the poor with supplementary income and make them self-reliant.

Fig. 13.5

What I object to, is the craze for machinery as such. The craze is for what they call labour-saving machinery. Men go on "saving labour", till thousands are without work and thrown on the open streets to die of starvation. I want to save time and labour, not for a fraction of mankind, but for all; I want the concentration of wealth, not in the hands of few, but in the hands of all.

YOUNG INDIA, 13 NOVEMBER 1924

Khaddar does not seek to destroy all machinery but it does regulate its use and check its weedy growth. It uses machinery for the service of the poorest in their own cottages. The wheel is itself an exquisite piece of machinery.

YOUNG INDIA, 17 MARCH 1927

This is how a Hindi newspaper in Gorakhpur reported the atmosphere during his speeches:

> At Bhatni Gandhiji addressed the local public and then the train started for Gorakhpur. There were not less than 15,000 to 20,000 people at Nunkhar, Deoria, Gauri Bazar, Chauri Chaura and Kusmhi (stations) ... Mahatmaji was very pleased to witness the scene at Kusmhi, as despite the fact that the station is in the middle of a jungle there were not less than 10,000 people here. Some, overcome with their love, were seen to be crying. At Deoria people wanted to give *bhent* (donations) to Gandhiji, but he asked them to give these at Gorakhpur. But at Chauri Chaura one Marwari gentleman managed to hand over something to him. Then there was no stopping. A sheet was spread and currency notes and coins started raining. It was a sight ... Outside the Gorakhpur station the Mahatma was stood on a high carriage and people had a good darshan of him for a couple of minutes.

Wherever Gandhiji went, rumours spread of his miraculous powers. In some places it was said that he had been sent by the King to redress the grievances of the farmers, and that he had the power to overrule all local officials. In other places it was claimed that Gandhiji's power was superior to that of the English monarch, and that with his arrival the colonial rulers would flee the district. There were also stories reporting dire consequences for those who opposed him; rumours spread of how villagers who criticised Gandhiji found their houses mysteriously falling apart or their crops failing.

Known variously as "Gandhi baba", "Gandhi Maharaj", or simply as "Mahatma", Gandhiji appea to the Indian peasant as a saviour, who would rescue them from high taxes and oppressive officials and restore dignity and autonomy to their lives. Gandhiji's appeal among the poor, and peasants in particular, was enhanced by his ascetic lifestyle, and by his shrewd use of symbols such as the *dhoti* and the *charkha*. Mahatma Gandhi was by caste a merchant, and by profession a lawyer; but his simple lifestyle and love of working with his hands allowed him to empathise more fully with the labouring poor and for them, in turn, to empathise with him. Where most

Source 2

The miraculous and the unbelievable

Local newspapers in the United Provinces recorded many of the rumours that circulated at that time. There were rumours that every person who wanted to test the power of the Mahatma had been surprised:

1. Sikandar Sahu from a village in Basti said on 15 February that he would believe in the Mahatmaji when the *karah* (boiling pan) full of sugar cane juice in his *karkhana* (where *gur* was produced) split into two. Immediately the *karah* actually split into two from the middle.

2. A cultivator in Azamgarh said that he would believe in the Mahatmaji's authenticity if sesamum sprouted on his field planted with wheat. Next day all the wheat in that field became sesamum.

contd

Source 2 (contd)

There were rumours that those who opposed Mahatma Gandhi invariably met with some tragedy.

1. A gentleman from Gorakhpur city questioned the need to ply the *charkha*. His house caught fire.

2. In April 1921 some people were gambling in a village of Uttar Pradesh. Someone told them to stop. Only one from amongst the group refused to stop and abused Gandhiji. The next day his goat was bitten by four of his own dogs.

3. In a village in Gorakhpur, the peasants resolved to give up drinking liquor. One person did not keep his promise. As soon as he started for the liquor shop brickbats started to rain in his path. When he spoke the name of Gandhiji the brickbats stopped flying.

FROM SHAHID AMIN, "GANDHI AS MAHATMA", *SUBALTERN STUDIES III*, OXFORD UNIVERSITY PRESS, DELHI.

➲ You have read about rumours in Chapter 11 and seen that the circulation of rumours tells us about the structure of the belief of a time: they tell us about the mind of the people who believe in the rumours and the circumstances that make this belief possible. What do you think these rumours about Gandhiji reflect?

other politicians talked down to them, Gandhiji appeared not just to look like them, but to understand them and relate to their lives.

While Mahatma Gandhi's mass appeal was undoubtedly genuine – and in the context of Indian politics, without precedent – it must also be stressed that his success in broadening the basis of nationalism was based on careful organisation. New branches of the Congress were set up in various parts of India. A series of "Praja Mandals" were established to promote the nationalist creed in the princely states. Gandhiji encouraged the communication of the nationalist message in the mother tongue, rather than in the language of the rulers, English. Thus the provincial committees of the Congress were based on linguistic regions, rather than on the artificial boundaries of British India. In these different ways nationalism was taken to the farthest corners of the country and embraced by social groups previously untouched by it.

By now, among the supporters of the Congress were some very prosperous businessmen and industrialists. Indian entrepreneurs were quick to recognise that, in a free India, the favours enjoyed by their British competitors would come to an end. Some of these entrepreneurs, such as G.D. Birla, supported the national movement openly; others did so tacitly. Thus, among Gandhiji's admirers were both poor peasants and rich industrialists, although the reasons why peasants followed Gandhiji were somewhat different from, and perhaps opposed to, the reasons of the industrialists.

While Mahatma Gandhi's own role was vital, the growth of what we might call "Gandhian nationalism" also depended to a very substantial extent on his followers. Between 1917 and 1922, a group of highly talented Indians attached themselves to Gandhiji. They included Mahadev Desai, Vallabh Bhai Patel, J.B. Kripalani, Subhas Chandra Bose, Abul Kalam Azad, Jawaharlal Nehru, Sarojini Naidu, Govind Ballabh Pant and C. Rajagopalachari. Notably, these close associates of Gandhiji came from different regions as well as different religious traditions. In turn, they inspired countless other Indians to join the Congress and work for it.

Mahatma Gandhi was released from prison in February 1924, and now chose to devote his attention to the promotion of home-spun cloth (*khadi*), and the abolition of untouchability. For, Gandhiji was as much a social reformer as he was a politician. He believed that in order to be worthy of freedom, Indians had to get rid of social evils such as child marriage and untouchability. Indians of one faith had also to cultivate a genuine tolerance for Indians of another – hence his emphasis on Hindu-Muslim harmony. Meanwhile, on the economic front Indians had to learn to become self-reliant – hence his stress on the significance of wearing *khadi* rather than mill-made cloth imported from overseas.

3. THE SALT SATYAGRAHA
A CASE STUDY

For several years after the Non-cooperation Movement ended, Mahatma Gandhi focused on his social reform work. In 1928, however, he began to think of re-entering politics. That year there was an all-India campaign in opposition to the all-White Simon Commission, sent from England to enquire into conditions in the colony. Gandhiji did not himself participate in this movement, although he gave it his blessings, as he also did to a peasant satyagraha in Bardoli in the same year.

In the end of December 1929, the Congress held its annual session in the city of Lahore. The meeting was significant for two things: the election of Jawaharlal Nehru as President, signifying the passing of the baton of leadership to the younger generation; and the proclamation of commitment to "Purna Swaraj", or complete independence. Now the pace of politics picked up once more. On 26 January 1930, "Independence Day" was observed, with the national flag being hoisted in different venues, and patriotic songs being sung. Gandhiji himself issued precise instructions as to how the day should be observed. "It would be good," he said, "if the declaration [of Independence] is made by whole villages, whole cities even ... It would be well if all the meetings were held at the identical minute in all the places."

Gandhiji suggested that the time of the meeting be advertised in the traditional way, by the beating of drums. The celebrations would begin with the hoisting of the national flag. The rest of the day would be spent "in doing some constructive work, whether it is spinning, or service of 'untouchables', or reunion of Hindus and Mussalmans, or prohibition work, or even all these

Discuss...
What was Non-cooperation? Find out about the variety of ways in which different social groups participated in the movement.

together, which is not impossible". Participants would take a pledge affirming that it was "the inalienable right of the Indian people, as of any other people, to have freedom and to enjoy the fruits of their toil", and that "if any government deprives a people of these rights and oppresses them, the people have a further right to alter it or abolish it".

3.1 Dandi

Soon after the observance of this "Independence Day", Mahatma Gandhi announced that he would lead a march to break one of the most widely disliked laws in British India, which gave the state a monopoly in the manufacture and sale of salt. His picking on the salt monopoly was another illustration of Gandhiji's tactical wisdom. For in every Indian household, salt was indispensable; yet people were forbidden from making salt even for domestic use, compelling them to buy it from shops at a high price. The state monopoly over salt was deeply unpopular; by making it his target, Gandhiji hoped to mobilise a wider discontent against British rule.

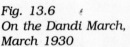

Fig. 13.6
On the Dandi March,
March 1930

Where most Indians understood the significance of Gandhiji's challenge, the British Raj apparently did not. Although Gandhiji had given advance notice of his "Salt March" to the Viceroy Lord Irwin, Irwin failed to grasp the significance of the action. On 12 March 1930, Gandhiji began walking from his ashram at Sabarmati towards the ocean. He reached his destination three weeks later, making a fistful of salt as he did and thereby making himself a criminal in the eyes of the law. Meanwhile, parallel salt marches were being conducted in other parts of the country.

Fig. 13.7
Satyagrahis picking up natural salt at the end of the Dandi March, 6 April 1930

Source 3

Why the Salt Satyagraha?

Why was salt the symbol of protest? This is what Mahatma Gandhi wrote:

The volume of information being gained daily shows how wickedly the salt tax has been designed. In order to prevent the use of salt that has not paid the tax which is at times even fourteen times its value, the Government destroys the salt it cannot sell profitably. Thus it taxes the nation's vital necessity; it prevents the public from manufacturing it and destroys what nature manufactures without effort. No adjective is strong enough for characterising this wicked dog-in-the-manger policy. From various sources I hear tales of such wanton destruction of the nation's property in all parts of India. Maunds if not tons of salt are said to be destroyed on the Konkan coast. The same tale comes from Dandi. Wherever there is likelihood of natural salt being taken away by the people living in the neighbourhood of such areas for their personal use, salt officers are posted for the sole purpose of carrying on destruction. Thus valuable national property is destroyed at national expense and salt taken out of the mouths of the people.

The salt monopoly is thus a fourfold curse. It deprives the people of a valuable easy village industry, involves wanton destruction of property that nature produces in abundance, the destruction itself means more national expenditure, and fourthly, to crown this folly, an unheard-of tax of more than 1,000 per cent is exacted from a starving people.

This tax has remained so long because of the apathy of the general public. Now that it is sufficiently roused, the tax has to go. How soon it will be abolished depends upon the strength the people.

THE COLLECTED WORKS OF MAHATMA GANDHI (CWMG), VOL. 49

➲ Why was salt destroyed by the colonial government? Why did Mahatma Gandhi consider the salt tax more oppressive than other taxes?

Source 4

"Tomorrow we shall break the salt tax law"

On 5 April 1930, Mahatma Gandhi spoke at Dandi:

When I left Sabarmati with my companions for this seaside hamlet of Dandi, I was not certain in my mind that we would be allowed to reach this place. Even while I was at Sabarmati there was a rumour that I might be arrested. I had thought that the Government might perhaps let my party come as far as Dandi, but not me certainly. If someone says that this betrays imperfect faith on my part, I shall not deny the charge. That I have reached here is in no small measure due to the power of peace and non-violence: that power is universally felt. The Government may, if it wishes, congratulate itself on acting as it has done, for it could have arrested every one of us. In saying that it did not have the courage to arrest this army of peace, we praise it. It felt ashamed to arrest such an army. He is a civilised man who feels ashamed to do anything which his neighbours would disapprove. The Government deserves to be congratulated on not arresting us, even if it desisted only from fear of world opinion.

Tomorrow we shall break the salt tax law. Whether the Government will tolerate that is a different question. It may not tolerate it, but it deserves congratulations on the patience and forbearance it has displayed in regard to this party. ...

What if I and all the eminent leaders in Gujarat and in the rest of the country are arrested? This movement is based on the faith that when a whole nation is roused and on the march no leader is necessary.

CWMG, VOL. 49

⊃ What does the speech tell us about how Gandhiji saw the colonial state?

As with Non-cooperation, apart from the officially sanctioned nationalist campaign, there were numerous other streams of protest. Across large parts of India, peasants breached the hated colonial forest laws that kept them and their cattle out of the woods in which they had once roamed freely. In some towns, factory workers went on strike while lawyers boycotted British courts and students refused to attend government-run educational institutions. As in 1920-22, now too Gandhiji's call had encouraged Indians of all classes to make manifest their own discontent with colonial rule. The rulers responded by detaining the dissenters. In the wake of the Salt March, nearly 60,000 Indians were arrested, among them, of course, Gandhiji himself.

The progress of Gandhiji's march to the seashore can be traced from the secret reports filed by the police officials deputed to monitor his movements. These reproduce the speeches he gave at the villages en route, in which he called upon local officials to renounce government employment and join the freedom struggle. In one village,

Wasna, Gandhiji told the upper castes that "if you are out for Swaraj you must serve untouchables. You won't get Swaraj merely by the repeal of the salt taxes or other taxes. For Swaraj you must make amends for the wrongs which you did to the untouchables. For Swaraj, Hindus, Muslims, Parsis and Sikhs will have to unite. These are the steps towards Swaraj." The police spies reported that Gandhiji's meetings were very well attended, by villagers of all castes, and by women as well as men. They observed that thousands of volunteers were flocking to the nationalist cause. Among them were many officials, who had resigned from their posts with the colonial government. Writing to the government, the District Superintendent of Police remarked, "Mr Gandhi appeared calm and collected. He is gathering more strength as he proceeds."

The progress of the Salt March can also be traced from another source: the American newsmagazine, *Time*. This, to begin with, scorned at Gandhiji's looks, writing with disdain of his "spindly frame" and his "spidery loins". Thus in its first report on the march, *Time* was deeply sceptical of the Salt March reaching its destination. It claimed that Gandhiji "sank to the ground" at the end of the second day's walking; the magazine did not believe that "the emaciated saint would be physically able to go much further". But within a week it had changed its mind. The massive popular following that the march had garnered, wrote *Time*, had made the British rulers "desperately anxious". Gandhiji himself they now

Fig. 13.8
After Mahatma Gandhi's release from prison in January 1931, Congress leaders met at Allahabad to plan the future course of action.
You can see (from right to left) Jawaharlal Nehru, Jamnalal Bajaj, Subhas Chandra Bose, Gandhiji, Mahadev Desai (in front), Sardar Vallabh Bhai Patel.

The problem with separate electorates

At the Round Table Conference Mahatma Gandhi stated his arguments against separate electorates for the Depressed Classes:

Separate electorates to the "Untouchables" will ensure them bondage in perpetuity ... Do you want the "Untouchables" to remain "Untouchables" for ever? Well, the separate electorates would perpetuate the stigma. What is needed is destruction of "Untouchability", and when you have done it, the bar-sinister, which has been imposed by an insolent "superior" class upon an "inferior" class will be destroyed. When you have destroyed the bar-sinister to whom will you give the separate electorates?

saluted as a "Saint" and "Statesman", who was using "Christian acts as a weapon against men with Christian beliefs".

3.2 Dialogues

The Salt March was notable for at least three reasons. First, it was this event that first brought Mahatma Gandhi to world attention. The march was widely covered by the European and American press. Second, it was the first nationalist activity in which women participated in large numbers. The socialist activist Kamaladevi Chattopadhyay had persuaded Gandhiji not to restrict the protests to men alone. Kamaladevi was herself one of numerous women who courted arrest by breaking the salt or liquor laws. Third, and perhaps most significant, it was the Salt March which forced upon the British the realisation that their Raj would not last forever, and that they would have to devolve some power to the Indians.

To that end, the British government convened a series of "Round Table Conferences" in London. The first meeting was held in November 1930, but without the pre-eminent political leader in India, thus rendering it an exercise in futility. Gandhiji was released from jail in January 1931 and the following month had several long meetings with the Viceroy. These culminated in what was called the "Gandhi-Irwin Pact', by the terms of which civil disobedience would be called off, all prisoners released, and salt manufacture allowed along the coast. The pact was criticised by radical nationalists, for Gandhiji was unable to obtain from the Viceroy a commitment to political independence for Indians; he could obtain merely an assurance of talks towards that possible end.

A second Round Table Conference was held in London in the latter part of 1931. Here, Gandhiji represented the Congress. However, his claims that his party represented all of India came under challenge from three parties: from the Muslim League, which claimed to stand for the interests of the Muslim minority; from the Princes, who claimed that the Congress had no stake in their territories; and from the brilliant lawyer and thinker B.R. Ambedkar, who argued that Gandhiji and the Congress did not really represent the lowest castes.

The Conference in London was inconclusive, so Gandhiji returned to India and resumed civil disobedience. The new Viceroy, Lord Willingdon, was deeply unsympathetic to the Indian leader. In a private

Fig. 13.9
At the Second Round Table Conference, London, November 1931
Mahatma Gandhi opposed the demand for separate
electorates for "lower castes". He believed that this would
prevent their integration into mainstream society and
permanently segregate them from other caste Hindus.

letter to his sister, Willingdon wrote: "It's a beautiful
world if it wasn't for Gandhi ... At the bottom of
every move he makes which he always says is
inspired by God, one discovers the political
manouevre. I see the American Press is saying what
a wonderful man he is ... But the fact is that we
live in the midst of very unpractical, mystical, and
superstitious folk who look upon Gandhi as
something holy, ..."

In 1935, however, a new Government of India Act
promised some form of representative government.
Two years later, in an election held on the basis
of a restricted franchise, the Congress won a
comprehensive victory. Now eight out of 11 provinces
had a Congress "Prime Minister", working under the
supervision of a British Governor.

In September 1939, two years after the Congress
ministries assumed office, the Second World War
broke out. Mahatma Gandhi and Jawaharlal Nehru
had both been strongly critical of Hitler and the
Nazis. Accordingly, they promised Congress support
to the war effort if the British, in return, promised
to grant India independence once hostilities ended.

Source 6

Ambedkar on separate electorates

In response to Mahatma
Gandhi's opposition to the
demand for separate electorates
for the Depressed Classes,
Ambedkar wrote:

Here is a class which is
undoubtedly not in a
position to sustain itself in
the struggle for existence.
The religion, to which they
are tied, instead of providing
them an honourable place,
brands them as lepers, not
fit for ordinary intercourse.
Economically, it is a class
entirely dependent upon
the high-caste Hindus for
earning its daily bread with
no independent way of living
open to it. Nor are all ways
closed by reason of the social
prejudices of the Hindus but
there is a definite attempt
all through our Hindu
Society to bolt every possible
door so as not to allow the
Depressed Classes any
opportunity to rise in the
scale of life.

In these circumstances, it
would be granted by all fair-
minded persons that as the
only path for a community
so handicapped to succeed
in the struggle for life against
organised tyranny, some
share of political power in
order that it may protect itself
is a paramount necessity ...

FROM DR BABASAHEB AMBEDKAR,
"WHAT CONGRESS AND GANDHI
HAVE DONE TO THE UNTOUCHABLES",
WRITINGS AND SPEECHES, VOL. 9, P. 312

Fig. 13.10
Mahatma Gandhi and Rajendra Prasad on their way to a meeting with the Viceroy, Lord Linlithgow, 13 October 1939
In the meeting the nature of India's involvement in the War was discussed. When negotiations with the Viceroy broke down, the Congress ministries resigned.

The offer was refused. In protest, the Congress ministries resigned in October 1939. Through 1940 and 1941, the Congress organised a series of individual satyagrahas to pressure the rulers to promise freedom once the war had ended.

Meanwhile, in March 1940, the Muslim League passed a resolution demanding a measure of autonomy for the Muslim-majority areas of the subcontinent. The political landscape was now becoming complicated: it was no longer Indians versus the British; rather, it had become a three-way struggle between the Congress, the Muslim League, and the British. At this time Britain had an all-party government, whose Labour members were sympathetic to Indian aspirations, but whose Conservative Prime Minister, Winston Churchill, was a diehard imperialist who insisted that he had not been appointed the King's First Minister in order to preside over the liquidation of the British Empire. In the spring of 1942, Churchill was persuaded to send one of his ministers, Sir Stafford Cripps, to India to try and forge a compromise with Gandhiji and the Congress. Talks broke down, however, after the Congress insisted that if it was to help the British defend India from the Axis powers, then the Viceroy had first to appoint an Indian as the Defence Member of his Executive Council.

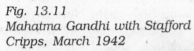

Fig. 13.11
Mahatma Gandhi with Stafford Cripps, March 1942

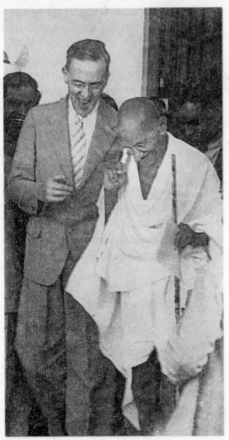

○ Discuss...
Read Sources 5 and 6. Write an imaginary dialogue between Ambedkar and Mahatma Gandhi on the issue of separate electorates for the Depressed Classes.

4. QUIT INDIA

After the failure of the Cripps Mission, Mahatma Gandhi decided to launch his third major movement against British rule. This was the "Quit India" campaign, which began in August 1942. Although Gandhiji was jailed at once, younger activists organised strikes and acts of sabotage all over the country. Particularly active in the underground resistance were socialist members of the Congress, such as Jayaprakash Narayan. In several districts, such as Satara in the west and Medinipur in the east, "independent" governments were proclaimed. The British responded with much force, yet it took more than a year to suppress the rebellion.

"Quit India" was genuinely a *mass* movement, bringing into its ambit hundreds of thousands of ordinary Indians. It especially energised the young who, in very large numbers, left their colleges to go to jail. However, while the Congress leaders languished in jail, Jinnah and his colleagues in the Muslim League worked patiently at expanding their influence. It was in these years that the League began to make a mark in the Punjab and Sind, provinces where it had previously had scarcely any presence.

In June 1944, with the end of the war in sight, Gandhiji was released from prison. Later that year

Satara, 1943

From the late nineteenth century, a non-Brahman movement, which opposed the caste system and landlordism, had developed in Maharashtra. This movement established links with the national movement by the 1930s.

In 1943, some of the younger leaders in the Satara district of Maharashtra set up a parallel government *(prati sarkar)*, with volunteer corps *(seba dals)* and village units *(tufan dals)*. They ran people's courts and organised constructive work. Dominated by *kunbi* peasants and supported by dalits, the Satara *prati sarkar* functioned till the elections of 1946, despite government repression and, in the later stages, Congress disapproval.

Fig. 13.12
Women's procession in Bombay during the Quit India Movement

he held a series of meetings with Jinnah, seeking to bridge the gap between the Congress and the League. In 1945, a Labour government came to power in Britain and committed itself to granting independence to India. Meanwhile, back in India, the Viceroy, Lord Wavell, brought the Congress and the League together for a series of talks.

Early in 1946 fresh elections were held to the provincial legislatures. The Congress swept the "General" category, but in the seats specifically reserved for Muslims the League won an overwhelming majority. The political polarisation was complete. A Cabinet Mission sent in the summer of 1946 failed to get the Congress and the League to agree on a federal system that would keep India together while allowing the provinces a degree of autonomy. After the talks broke down, Jinnah called for a "Direct Action Day" to press the League's demand for Pakistan. On the designated day, 16 August 1946, bloody riots broke out in Calcutta. The violence spread to rural Bengal, then to Bihar, and then across the country to the United Provinces and the Punjab. In some places, Muslims were the main sufferers, in other places, Hindus.

In February 1947, Wavell was replaced as Viceroy by Lord Mountbatten. Mountbatten called one last round of talks, but when these too proved inconclusive he announced that British India would be freed, but also divided. The formal transfer of power was fixed for 15 August. When that day came, it was celebrated with gusto in different parts of India. In Delhi, there was "prolonged applause" when the President of the Constituent Assembly began the meeting by invoking the Father of the Nation – Mohandas Karamchand Gandhi. Outside the Assembly, the crowds shouted "Mahatma Gandhi ki jai".

Fig. 13.13
Mahatma Gandhi conferring with Jawaharlal Nehru (on his right) and Sardar Vallabh Bhai Patel (on his left) Nehru and Patel represented two distinct political tendencies within the Congress – the socialist and the conservative. Mahatma Gandhi had to often mediate between these groups.

5. THE LAST HEROIC DAYS

As it happened, Mahatma Gandhi was not present at
the festivities in the capital on 15 August 1947. He
was in Calcutta, but he did not attend any function or
hoist a flag there either. Gandhiji marked the day with
a 24-hour fast. The freedom he had struggled so long
for had come at an unacceptable price, with a nation
divided and Hindus and Muslims at each other's throats.

Through September and October, writes his
biographer D.G. Tendulkar, Gandhiji "went round
hospitals and refugee camps giving consolation to
distressed people". He "appealed to the Sikhs, the
Hindus and the Muslims to forget the past and not
to dwell on their sufferings but to extend the right
hand of fellowship to each other, and to determine
to live in peace ..."

At the initiative of Gandhiji and Nehru, the Congress
now passed a resolution on "the rights of minorities".
The party had never accepted the "two-nation theory":
forced against its will to accept Partition, it still believed
that "India is a land of many religions and many races,
and must remain so". Whatever be the situation in
Pakistan, India would be "a democratic secular State
where all citizens enjoy full rights and are equally
entitled to the protection of the State, irrespective of
the religion to which they belong". The Congress wished
to "assure the minorities in India that it will continue
to protect, to the best of its ability, their citizen rights
against aggression".

Many scholars have written of the months after
Independence as being Gandhiji's "finest hour". After
working to bring peace to Bengal,
Gandhiji now shifted to Delhi, from
where he hoped to move on to the riot-
torn districts of Punjab. While in the
capital, his meetings were disrupted
by refugees who objected to readings
from the Koran, or shouted slogans
asking why he did not speak of the
sufferings of those Hindus and Sikhs
still living in Pakistan. In fact, as
D.G. Tendulkar writes, Gandhiji "was
equally concerned with the sufferings
of the minority community in
Pakistan. He would have liked to be
able to go to their succour. But with

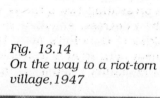

Fig. 13.14
On the way to a riot-torn
village, 1947

Fig. 13.15
*The death of the Mahatma,
a popular print*
In popular representations,
Mahatma Gandhi was deified,
and shown as the unifying force
within the national movement.
Here you can see Jawaharlal
Nehru and Sardar Patel,
representing two strands within
the Congress, standing on two
sides of Gandhiji's pyre. Blessing
them both from a heavenly realm,
is Mahatma Gandhi, at the centre.

what face could he now go there, when he could not guarantee full redress to the Muslims in Delhi?"

There was an attempt on Gandhiji's life on 20 January 1948, but he carried on undaunted. On 26 January, he spoke at his prayer meeting of how that day had been celebrated in the past as Independence Day. Now freedom had come, but its first few months had been deeply disillusioning. However, he trusted that "the worst is over", that Indians would henceforth work collectively for the "equality of all classes and creeds, never the domination and superiority of the major community over a minor, however insignificant it may be in numbers or influence". He also permitted himself the hope "that though geographically and politically India is divided into two, at heart we shall ever be friends and brothers helping and respecting one another and be one for the outside world".

Gandhiji had fought a lifelong battle for a free and united India; and yet, when the country was divided, he urged that the two parts respect and befriend one another.

Other Indians were less forgiving. At his daily prayer meeting on the evening of 30 January, Gandhiji was shot dead by a young man. The assassin, who surrendered afterwards, was a Brahmin from Pune named Nathuram Godse, the editor of an extremist Hindu newspaper who had denounced Gandhiji as "an appeaser of Muslims".

Gandhiji's death led to an extraordinary outpouring of grief, with rich tributes being paid to him from across the political spectrum in India, and moving appreciations coming from such international figures as George Orwell and Albert Einstein. *Time* magazine, which had once mocked Gandhiji's physical size and seemingly non-rational ideas, now compared his martyrdom to that of Abraham Lincoln: it was a bigoted American who had killed Lincoln for believing that human beings were equal regardless of their race or skin colour; and it was a bigoted Hindu who had killed Gandhiji for believing that friendship was possible, indeed necessary, between Indians of different faiths. In this respect, as *Time* wrote, "The world knew that it had, in a sense too deep, too simple for the world to understand, connived at his (Gandhiji's) death as it had connived at Lincoln's."

6. KNOWING GANDHI

There are many different kinds of sources from which we can reconstruct the political career of Gandhiji and the history of the nationalist movement.

6.1 Public voice and private scripts

One important source is the writings and speeches of Mahatma Gandhi and his contemporaries, including both his associates and his political adversaries. Within these writings we need to distinguish between those that were meant for the public and those that were not. Speeches, for instance, allow us to hear the public voice of an individual, while private letters give us a glimpse of his or her private thoughts. In letters we see people expressing their anger and pain, their dismay and anxiety, their hopes and frustrations in ways in which they may not express themselves in public statements. But we must remember that this private-public distinction often breaks down. Many letters are written to individuals, and are therefore personal, but they are also meant for the public. The language of the letters is often shaped by the awareness that they may one day be published. Conversely, the fear that a letter may get into print often prevents people from expressing their opinion freely in personal letters. Mahatma Gandhi regularly published in his journal, *Harijan*, letters that others wrote to him. Nehru edited a collection of letters written to him during the national movement and published *A Bunch of Old Letters*.

Source 7

One event through letters

In the 1920s, Jawaharlal Nehru was increasingly influenced by socialism, and he returned from Europe in 1928 deeply impressed with the Soviet Union. As he began working closely with the socialists (Jayaprakash Narayan, Narendra Dev, N.G. Ranga and others), a rift developed between the socialists and the conservatives within the Congress. After becoming the Congress President in 1936, Nehru spoke passionately against fascism, and upheld the demands of workers and peasants.

Worried by Nehru's socialist rhetoric, the conservatives, led by Rajendra Prasad and Sardar Patel, threatened to resign from the Working Committee, and some prominent industrialists in Bombay issued a statement attacking Nehru. Both Prasad and Nehru turned to Mahatma Gandhi and met him at his ashram at Wardha. The latter acted as the mediator, as he often did, restraining Nehru's radicalism and persuading Prasad and others to see the significance of Nehru's leadership.

In *A Bunch of Old Letters*, 1958, Nehru reprinted many of the letters that were exchanged at the time.

Read the extracts in the following pages.

Source 7 (contd)

My dear Jawaharlalji,   *Wardha, July 1, 1936*

Since we parted yesterday we have had a long conversation with Mahatmaji and a prolonged consultation among ourselves. We understand that you have felt much hurt by the course of action taken by us and particularly the tone of our letter has caused you much pain. It was never our intention either to embarrass you or to hurt you and if you had suggested or indictated that it hurt you we would have without the least hesitation amended or altered the letter. But we have decided to withdraw it and our resignation on a reconsideration of the whole situation.

We have felt that in all your utterances as published in the Press you have been speaking not so much on the general Congress programme as on a topic which has not been accepted by the Congress and in doing so you have been acting more as the mouthpiece of the minority of our colleagues on the Working Committee as also on the Congress than the mouthpiece of the majority which we expected you as Congress President to do.

There is regular continuous campaign against us treating us as persons whose time is over, who represent and stand for ideas that are worn out and that have no present value, who are only obstructing the progress of the country and who deserve to be cast out of the positions which they undeservedly hold ... we have felt that a great injustice has been and is being done to us by others, and we are not receiving the protection we are entitled from you as our colleague and as our President ...

Yours sincerely
Rajendra Prasad

My Dear Bapu,   *Allahabad, July 5, 1936*

I arrived here last night. Ever since I left Wardha I have been feeling weak in body and troubled in mind.
    ... Since my return from Europe, I found that meetings of the Working Committee exhaust me greatly; they have a devitalising effect on me and I have almost the feeling of being older in years after every fresh experience ...

I am grateful to you for all the trouble you took in smoothing over matters and in helping to avoid a crisis.

I read again Rajendra Babu's letter to me (the second one) and his formidable indictment of me ...

For however tenderly the fact may be stated, it amounts to this that I am an intolerable nuisance and the very qualities I possess – a measure of ability, energy, earnestness, some personality which has a vague appeal – become dangerous for they are harnessed to the wrong chariot (socialism). The conclusion from all this is obvious.

I have written at length, both in my book and subsequently, about my present ideas. There is no lack of material for me to be judged. Those views are not casual. They are part of me, and though I might change them or vary them in future, so long as I hold them I must give expression to them. Because I attached importance to a larger unity I tried to express them in the mildest way possible and more as an invitation to thought than as fixed conclusions. I saw no conflict in this approach and in anything that the Congress was doing. So far as the elections were concerned I felt that my approach was a definite asset to us as it enthused the masses. But my approach, mild and vague as it was, is considered dangerous and harmful by my colleagues. I was even told that my laying stress always on the poverty and unemployment in India was unwise, or at any rate the way I did it was wrong ...

You told me that you intended issuing some kind of a statement. I shall welcome this for I believe in every viewpoint being placed before the country.

Yours affectionately
Jawaharlal

Source 7 (contd)

Segaon, July 15, 1936

Dear Jawaharlal,

Your letter is touching. You feel the most injured party. The fact is that your colleagues have lacked your courage and frankness. The result has been disastrous. I have always pleaded with them to speak to you freely and fearlessly. But having lacked the courage, whenever they have spoken they have done it clumsily and you have felt irritated. I tell you they have dreaded you, because of your irritability and impatience with them. They have chafed under your rebukes and magisterial manner and above all your arrogation of what has appeared to them your infallibility and superior knowledge. They feel you have treated them with scant courtesy and never defended them from socialist ridicule and even misrepresentation.

I have looked at the whole affair as a tragi-comedy. I would therefore like you to look at the whole thing in a lighter vein.

I suggested your name for the crown of thorns (Presidentship of the Congress). Keep it on, though the head be bruised. Resume your humour at the committee meetings. That is your most usual role, not that of care-worn, irritable man ready to burst on the slightest occasion.

How I wish you could telegraph me that on finishing my letter you felt as merry as you were on that new year's day in Lahore when you were reported to have danced around the tricolour flag.

You must give your throat a chance.

Love
Bapu

> ➲
> (a) What do the letters tell us about the way Congress ideals developed over time?
> (b) What do they reveal about the role of Mahatma Gandhi within the national movement?
> (c) Do such letters give us any special insight into the working of the Congress, and into the nature of the national movement?

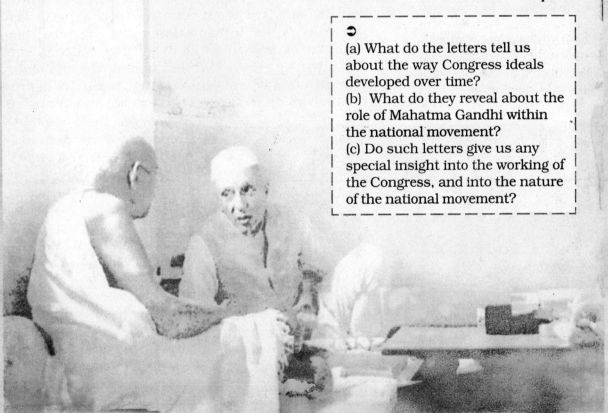

6.2 Framing a picture

Autobiographies similarly give us an account of the past that is often rich in human detail. But here again we have to be careful of the way we read and interpret autobiographies. We need to remember that they are retrospective accounts written very often from memory. They tell us what the author could recollect, what he or she saw as important, or was keen on recounting, or how a person wanted his or her life to be viewed by others. Writing an autobiography is a way of framing a picture of yourself. So in reading these accounts we have to try and see what the author does not tell us; we need to understand the reasons for that silence – those wilful or unwitting acts of forgetting.

6.3 Through police eyes

Another vital source is government records, for the colonial rulers kept close tabs on those they regarded as critical of the government. The letters and reports written by policemen and other officials were secret at the time; but now can be accessed in archives.

Let us look at one such source: the fortnightly reports that were prepared by the Home Department from the early twentieth century. These reports were based on police information from the localities, but often expressed what the higher officials saw, or wanted to believe. While noticing the possibility of sedition and rebellion, they liked to assure themselves that these fears were unwarranted. If you see the Fortnightly Reports for the period of the Salt March you will notice that the Home Department was unwilling to accept that Mahatma Gandhi's actions had evoked any enthusiastic response from the masses. The march was seen as a drama, an antic, a desperate effort to mobilise people who were unwilling to rise against the British and were busy with their daily schedules, happy under the Raj.

Fig. 13.16
Police clash with Congress volunteers in Bombay during the Civil Disobedience Movement.

➲ Can you see any conflict between this image and what was reported in the Fortnightly Reports of the police?

Source 8

Fortnightly Reports of the Home Department
(Confidential)

FOR THE FIRST HALF OF MARCH 1930

The rapid political developments in Gujarat are being closely watched here. To what extent and in what directions they will affect political condition in this province, it is difficult to surmise at present. The peasantry is for the moment engaged in harvesting a good rabi; students are pre-occupied with their impending examinations.

Central Provinces and Berar

The arrest of Mr. Vallabh Bhai Patel caused little excitement, except in Congress circles, but a meeting organised by the Nagpur Nagar Congress Committee to congratulate Gandhi on the start of his march was attended by a crowd of over 3000 people at Nagpur.

Bengal

The outstanding event of the past fortnight has been the start of Gandhi's campaign of civil disobedience. Mr. J.M. Sengupta has formed an All-Bengal Civil Disobedience Council, and the Bengal Provincial Congress Committee has formed an All Bengal Council of Disobedience. But beyond forming councils no active steps have yet been taken in the matter of civil disobedience in Bengal.

The reports from the districts show that the meetings that have been held excite little or no interest and leave no profound impression on the general population. It is noticeable, however, that ladies are attending these meetings in increasing numbers.

Bihar and Orissa

There is still little to report regarding Congress activity. There is a good deal of talk about a campaign to withhold payment of the chaukidari tax, but no area has yet been selected for experiment. The arrest of Gandhi is being foretold freely but it seems quite possible that nonfulfilment of the forecast is upsetting plans.

Madras

The opening of Gandhi's civil disobedience campaign has completely overshadowed all other issues. General opinion inclines to regard his march as theatrical and his programme as impracticable, but as he is held in such personal reverence by the Hindu public generally, the possibility of arrest which he seems deliberately to be courting and its effect on the political situation are viewed with considerable misgiving.

The 12th of March was celebrated as the day of inaugurating the civil disobedience campaign. In Bombay the celebrations took the form of saluting the national flag in the morning.

Bombay

Press *Kesari* indulged in offensive language and in its usual attitude of blowing hot and cold wrote: "If the Government wants to test the power of Satyagraha, both its action and inaction will cause injury to it. If it arrests Gandhi it will incur the discontent of the nation; if it does not do that, the movement of civil disobedience will go on spreading. We therefore say that if the Government punishes Mr. Gandhi the nation will have won a victory, and if it lets him alone it will have won a still greater victory."

On the other hand the moderate paper *Vividh Vritt* pointed out the futility of the movement and opined that it could not achieve the end in view. It, however, reminded the government that repression would defeat its purpose.

contd

Source 8 (contd)

FOR THE SECOND HALF OF MARCH 1930

Bengal

Interest has continued to centre round Gandhi's march to the sea and the arrangements which he is making to initiate a campaign of civil disobedience. The extremist papers report his doings and speeches at great length and make a great display of the various meetings that are being held throughout Bengal and the resolutions passed thereat. But there is little enthusiasm for the form of civil disobedience favoured by Gandhi …

Generally people are waiting to see what happens to Gandhi and the probability is that if any action is taken against him, a spark will be set to much inflammable material in Bengal. But the prospect of any serious conflagration is at present slight.

Central Provinces and Berar

In Nagpur these meetings were well attended and most of the schools and colleges were deserted on the 12th March to mark the inauguration of Gandhi's march.

The boycott of liquor shops and the infringement of forest laws appear to be the most probable line of attack.

Punjab

It seems not improbable that organised attempts will be made to break the Salt Law in the Jhelum district; that the agitation relating to the non-payment of the water-tax in Multan will be revived; and that some movement in connection with the National Flag will be started probably at Gujranwala.

United Provinces

Political activity has undoubtedly intensified during the last fortnight. The Congress party feels that it must do something spectacular to sustain public interest. Enrolment of volunteers, propaganda in villages, preparations for breaking the salt laws on receipt of Mr. Gandhi's orders are reported from a number of districts.

FOR THE FIRST HALF OF APRIL 1930

United Provinces

Events have moved rapidly during the fortnight. Apart from political meetings, processions and the enrolment of volunteers, the Salt Act has been openly defied at Agra, Cawnpore, Benaras, Allahabad, Lucknow, Meerut, Rae Bareli, Farukhabad, Etawah, Ballia and Mainpuri.

Pt. Jawaharlal Nehru was arrested at Cheoki railway station early on the morning of April 14 as he was proceeding to the Central Provinces to attend a meeting of Youth League. He was at once taken direct to Naini Central Jail, where he was tried and sentenced to six months simple imprisonment.

Bihar and Orissa

There have been, or are now materialising, spectacular, but small-scale, attempts at illicit salt manufacture in a few places …

Central Provinces

In Jubbalpore Seth Govinddass has attempted to manufacture chemical salt at a cost many times in excess of the market price of clean salt.

Madras

Considerable opposition was shown at Vizagapatam to the Police when they attempted to seize salt made by boiling sea water, but elsewhere resistance to the seizure of illicit salt has been half hearted.

Bengal

In the mufassal efforts have been made to manufacture illicit salt, the main operation areas being the districts of 24-Parganas and Midnapore.

Very little salt has actually been manufactured and most of it has been confiscated and the utensils in which it was manufactured destroyed.

⊃ Read the Fortnightly Reports carefully. Remember they are extracts from confidential reports of the colonial Home Department. These reports did not always accept what the police reported from different localities.

(1) How do you think the nature of the source affects what is being said in these reports? Write a short note illustrating your argument with quotations from the above text.

(2) Why do you think the Home Department was continuously reporting on what people thought about the possibility of Mahatma Gandhi's arrest? Reread what Gandhiji said about the question of arrests in his speech on 5 April 1930 at Dandi.

(3) Why do you think Mahatma Gandhi was not arrested?

(4) Why do you think the Home Department continued to say that the march was not evoking any response?

6.4 From newspapers

One more important source is contemporary newspapers, published in English as well as in the different Indian languages, which tracked Mahatma Gandhi's movements and reported on his activities, and also represented what ordinary Indians thought of him. Newspaper accounts, however, should not be seen as unprejudiced. They were published by people who had their own political opinions and world views. These ideas shaped what was published and the way events were reported. The accounts that were published in a London newspaper would be different from the report in an Indian nationalist paper.

We need to look at these reports but should be careful while interpreting them. Every statement made in these cannot be accepted literally as representing what was happening on the ground. They often reflect the fears and anxieties of officials who were unable to control a movement and were anxious about its spread. They did not know whether to arrest Mahatma Gandhi or what an arrest would mean. The more the colonial state kept a watch on the public and its activities, the more it worried about the basis of its rule.

Fig. 13.17
Pictures like this reveal how Mahatma Gandhi was perceived by people and represented in popular prints
Within the tree of nationalism, Mahatma Gandhi appears as the looming central figure surrounded by small images of other leaders and sages.

TIMELINE

1915	Mahatma Gandhi returns from South Africa
1917	Champaran movement
1918	Peasant movements in Kheda (Gujarat), and workers' movement in Ahmedabad
1919	Rowlatt Satyagraha (March-April)
1919	Jallianwala Bagh massacre (April)
1921	Non-cooperation and Khilafat Movements
1928	Peasant movement in Bardoli
1929	"Purna Swaraj" accepted as Congress goal at the Lahore Congress (December)
1930	Civil Disobedience Movement begins; Dandi March (March-April)
1931	Gandhi-Irwin Pact (March); Second Round Table Conference (December)
1935	Government of India Act promises some form of representative government
1939	Congress ministries resign
1942	Quit India Movement begins (August)
1946	Mahatma Gandhi visits Noakhali and other riot-torn areas to stop communal violence

ANSWER IN 100-150 WORDS

1. How did Mahatma Gandhi seek to identify with the common people?

2. How was Mahatma Gandhi perceived by the peasants?

3. Why did the salt laws become an important issue of struggle?

4. Why are newspapers an important source for the study of the national movement?

5. Why was the *charkha* chosen as a symbol of nationalism?

WRITE A SHORT ESSAY (250-300 WORDS) ON THE FOLLOWING:

6. How was non-cooperation a form of protest?

7. Why were the dialogues at the Round Table Conference inconclusive?

8. In what way did Mahatma Gandhi transform the nature of the national movement?

9. What do private letters and autobiographies tell us about an individual? How are these sources different from official accounts?

MAP WORK

10. Find out about the route of the Dandi March. On a map of Gujarat plot the line of the march and mark the major towns and villages that it passed along the route.

PROJECT (CHOOSE ONE)

11. Read any two autobiographies of nationalist leaders. Look at the different ways in which the authors represent their own life and times, and interpret the national movement. See how their views differ. Write an account based on your studies.

12. Choose any event that took place during the national movement. Try and read the letters and speeches of the leaders of the time. Some of these are now published. He could be a local leader from the region where you live. Try and see how the local leaders viewed the activities of the national leadership at the top. Write about the movement based on your reading.

If you would like to know more, read:

Sekhar Bandyopadhyay. 2004. *From Plassey to Partition: A History of Modern India.* Orient Longman, New Delhi.

Sarvepalli Gopal. 1975. *Jawaharlal Nehru: A Biography, Volume I, 1889-1947.* Oxford University Press, Delhi.

David Hardiman. 2003. *Gandhi in His Time and Ours.* Permanent Black, New Delhi.

Gyanendra Pandey. 1978. *The Ascendancy of the Congress in Uttar Pradesh. 1926-34.* Oxford University Press, Delhi.

Sumit Sarkar. 1983. *Modern India, 1885-1947.* Macmillan, New Delhi.

You could visit:
http:/www.gandhiserve.org/cwmg/cwmg.html
(for Collected Works of Mahatma Gandhi)

UNDERSTANDING PARTITION
POLITICS, MEMORIES, EXPERIENCES

Fig. 14.1
Partition uprooted millions, transforming them into refugees, forcing them to begin
life from scratch in new lands.

We know that the joy of our country's independence from colonial rule in 1947 was tarnished by the violence and brutality of Partition. The Partition of British India into the sovereign states of India and Pakistan (with its western and eastern wings) led to many sudden developments. Thousands of lives were snuffed out, many others changed dramatically, cities changed, India changed, a new country was born, and there was unprecedented genocidal violence and migration.

This chapter will examine the history of Partition: why and how it happened as well as the harrowing experiences of ordinary people during the period 1946-50 and beyond. It will also discuss how the history of these experiences can be reconstructed by talking to people and interviewing them, that is, through the use of oral history. At the same time, it will point out the strengths and limitations of oral history. Interviews can tell us about certain aspects of a society's past of which we may know very little or nothing from other types of sources. But they may not reveal very much about many matters whose history we would then need to build from other materials. We will return to this issue towards the end of the chapter.

Fig. 14.2
Photographs give us a glimpse of the violence of that time.

1. SOME PARTITION EXPERIENCES

Here are three incidents narrated by people who experienced those trying times to a researcher in 1993. The informants were Pakistanis, the researcher Indian. The job of this researcher was to understand how those who had lived more or less harmoniously for generations inflicted so much violence on each other in 1947.

Source 1

"I am simply returning my father's *karz*, his debt"

This is what the researcher recorded:

During my visits to the History Department Library of Punjab University, Lahore, in the winter of 1992, the librarian, Abdul Latif, a pious middle-aged man, would help me a lot. He would go out of his way, well beyond the call of duty, to provide me with relevant material, meticulously keeping photocopies requested by me ready before my arrival the following morning. I found his attitude to my work so extraordinary that one day I could not help asking him, "Latif Sahib, why do you go out of your way to help me so much?" Latif Sahib glanced at his watch, grabbed his *namazi topi* and said, "I must go for *namaz* right now but I will answer your question on my return." Stepping into his office half an hour later, he continued:

"Yes, your question. I … I mean, my father belonged to Jammu, to a small village in Jammu district. This was a Hindu-dominated village and Hindu ruffians of the area massacred the hamlet's Muslim population in August 1947. One late afternoon, when the Hindu mob had been at its furious worst, my father discovered he was perhaps the only Muslim youth of the village left alive. He had already lost his entire family in the butchery and was looking for ways of escaping. Remembering a kind, elderly Hindu lady, a neighbour, he implored her to save him by offering him shelter at her place. The lady agreed to help father but said, 'Son, if you hide here, they will get both of us. This is of no use. You follow me to the spot where they have piled up the dead. You lie down there *as if dead* and I will dump a few dead-bodies on you. Lie there among the dead, son, as if dead *through the night* and run for your life towards Sialkot at the break of dawn tomorrow.'

"My father agreed to the proposal. Off they went to that spot, father lay on the ground and the old lady dumped a number of bodies on him. An hour or so later a group of armed Hindu hoodlums appeared. One of them yelled, 'Any life left in anybody?' and the others started, with their crude staffs and guns, to feel for any trace of life in that heap. Somebody shouted, 'There is a wrist watch on that body!' and hit my father's fingers with the butt of his rifle. Father used to tell us how difficult it was for him to keep his outstretched palm, beneath the watch he was wearing, so utterly still. Somehow he succeeded for a few seconds until one of them said 'Oh, it's only a watch. Come let us leave, it is getting dark.' Fortunately, for Abbaji, they left and my father lay there in that wretchedness the whole night, literally running for his life at the first hint of light. He did not stop until he reached Sialkot.

"I help you because that Hindu *mai* helped my father. I am simply returning my father's *karz*, his debt."

"But I am *not* a Hindu," I said. "Mine is a Sikh family, at best a mixed Hindu-Sikh one."

"I do not know what your religion is with any surety. You do not wear uncut hair and you are not a Muslim. So, for me you are a Hindu and I do my little bit for you because a Hindu *mai* saved my father."

Source 2

"For quite a few years now, I have not met a Punjabi *Musalman*"

The researcher's second story is about the manager of a youth hostel in Lahore.

I had gone to the hostel looking for accommodation and had promptly declared my citizenship. "You are Indian, so I cannot allot you a room but I can offer you tea and a story," said the Manager. I couldn't have refused such a tempting offer. "In the early 1950s I was posted at Delhi," the Manager began. I was all ears:

"I was working as a clerk at the Pakistani High Commission there and I had been asked by a Lahori friend to deliver a *rukka* (a short handwritten note) to his erstwhile neighbour who now resided at Paharganj in Delhi. One day I rode out on my bicycle towards Paharganj and just as I crossed the cathedral at the Central Secretariat, spotting a Sikh cyclist I asked him in Punjabi, 'Sardarji, the way to Paharganj, please?'

'Are you a refugee?' he asked.

'No, I come from Lahore. I am Iqbal Ahmed.'

'Iqbal Ahmed ... from Lahore? Stop!'

"That 'Stop!' sounded like a brute order to me and I instantly thought now I'll be gone. This Sikh will finish me off. But there was no escaping the situation, so I stopped. The burly Sikh came running to me and gave me a mighty hug. Eyes moist, he said, 'For quite a few years now, I have not met a Punjabi *Musalman*. I have been longing to meet one but you cannot find Punjabi-speaking *Musalmans* here.'"

Fig. 14.3
Over 10 million people were uprooted from their homelands and forced to migrate.

Source 3

"No, no! You can never be ours"

This is the third story the researcher related:

I still vividly remember a man I met in Lahore in 1992. He mistook me to be a Pakistani studying abroad. For some reason he liked me. He urged me to return home after completing my studies to serve the *qaum* (nation). I told him I shall do so but, at some stage in the conversation, I added that my citizenship happens to be Indian. All of a sudden his tone changed, and much as he was restraining himself, he blurted out,

"Oh Indian! I had thought you were Pakistani." I tried my best to impress upon him that I always see myself as South Asian. "No, no! You can never be ours. Your people wiped out my entire village in 1947, we are sworn enemies and shall always remain so."

(1) What do each of these sources show about the attitudes of the men who were talking with each other?

(2) What do you think these stories reveal about the different memories that people carried about Partition?

(3) How did the men identify themselves and one another?

Discuss...

Assess the value of such stories in writing about Partition.

2. A MOMENTOUS MARKER

2.1 Partition or holocaust?

The narratives just presented point to the pervasive violence that characterised Partition. Several hundred thousand people were killed and innumerable women raped and abducted. Millions were uprooted, transformed into refugees in alien lands. It is impossible to arrive at any accurate estimate of casualties: informed and scholarly guesses vary from 200,000 to 500,000 people. In all probability, some 15 million had to move across hastily constructed frontiers separating India and Pakistan. As they stumbled across these "shadow lines" – the boundaries between the two new states were not officially known until two days *after* formal independence – they were rendered homeless, having suddenly lost all their immovable property and most of their movable assets, separated from many of their relatives and friends as well, torn asunder from their moorings, from their houses, fields and fortunes, from their childhood memories. Thus stripped of their local or regional cultures, they were forced to begin picking up their life from scratch.

Fig. 14.4
On carts with families and belongings, 1947

Was this simply a *partition*, a more or less orderly constitutional arrangement, an agreed-upon division of territories and assets? Or should it be called a sixteen-month civil war, recognising that there were well-organised forces on both sides and concerted attempts to wipe out entire populations as enemies? The survivors themselves have often spoken of 1947 through other words: "*maashal-la*" (martial law), "*mara-mari*" (killings), and "*raula*", or "*hullar*" (disturbance, tumult, uproar). Speaking of the killings, rape, arson, and loot that constituted Partition, contemporary observers and scholars have sometimes used the expression "holocaust" as well, primarily meaning destruction or slaughter on a mass scale.

Is this usage appropriate?

You would have read about the German Holocaust under the Nazis in Class IX. The term "holocaust" in a sense captures the gravity of what happened in the subcontinent in 1947, something that the mild term "partition" hides. It also helps to focus on why Partition, like the Holocaust in Germany, is *remembered* and referred to in our contemporary concerns so much. Yet, differences between the two events should not be overlooked. In 1947-48, the subcontinent did not witness any state-driven extermination as was the case with Nazi Germany where various modern techniques of control and organisation had been used. The "ethnic cleansing" that characterised the partition of India was carried out by self-styled representatives of religious communities rather than by state agencies.

2.2 The power of stereotypes

India-haters in Pakistan and Pakistan-haters in India are both products of Partition. At times, some people mistakenly believe that the loyalties of Indian Muslims lie with Pakistan. The stereotype of extra-territorial, pan-Islamic loyalties comes fused with other highly objectionable ideas: Muslims are cruel, bigoted, unclean, descendants of invaders, while Hindus are kind, liberal, pure, children of the invaded. The journalist R.M. Murphy has shown that similar stereotypes proliferate in Pakistan. According to him, some Pakistanis feel that Muslims are fair, brave, monotheists and meat-eaters, while Hindus are dark, cowardly, polytheists and vegetarian. Some of these stereotypes pre-date Partition but there is no doubt that they were immensely strengthened because of 1947. Every myth in these constructions has been systematically critiqued by historians. But in both countries voices of hatred do not mellow.

Partition generated memories, hatreds, stereotypes and identities that still continue to shape the history of people on both sides of the border. These hatreds have manifested themselves during inter-community conflicts, and communal clashes in turn have kept alive the memories of past violence. Stories of Partition violence are recounted by communal groups to deepen the divide between communities: creating in people's minds feelings of suspicion and distrust, consolidating the power of communal stereotypes, creating the deeply problematic notion that Hindus, Sikhs and Muslims are communities with sharply defined boundaries, and fundamentally opposed interests.

The relationship between Pakistan and India has been profoundly shaped by this legacy of Partition. Perceptions of communities on both sides have been structured by the conflicting memories of those momentous times.

➲ **Discuss...**
Recall some stories of Partition you may have heard. Think of the way these have shaped your conception about different communities.
Try and imagine how the same stories would be narrated by different communities.

Fig. 14.5
People took with them only what they could physically carry.
Uprooting meant an immense sense of loss, a rupture with the place they had lived in for generations.

3. WHY AND HOW DID PARTITION HAPPEN?

3.1 Culminating point of a long history?

Some historians, both Indian and Pakistani, suggest that Mohammad Ali Jinnah's theory that the Hindus and Muslims in colonial India constituted two separate nations can be projected back into medieval history. They emphasise that the events of 1947 were intimately connected to the long history of Hindu-Muslim conflict throughout medieval and modern times. Such an argument does not recognise that the history of conflict between communities has coexisted with a long history of sharing, and of mutual cultural exchange. It also does not take into account the changing circumstances that shape people's thinking.

Some scholars see Partition as a culmination of a communal politics that started developing in the opening decades of the twentieth century. They suggest that separate electorates for Muslims, created by the colonial government in 1909 and expanded in 1919, crucially shaped the nature of communal politics. Separate electorates meant that Muslims could now elect their own representatives in designated constituencies. This created a temptation for politicians working within this system to use sectarian slogans and gather a following by distributing favours to their own religious groups. Religious identities thus acquired a functional use within a modern political system; and the logic of electoral politics deepened and hardened these identities. Community identities no longer indicated simple difference in faith and belief; they came to mean active opposition and hostility between communities. However, while separate electorates did have a profound impact on Indian politics, we should be careful not to over-emphasise their significance or to see Partition as a logical outcome of their working.

Communal identities were consolidated by a host of other developments in the early twentieth century. During the 1920s and early 1930s tension grew around a number of issues. Muslims were angered by "music-before-mosque", by the cow protection movement, and by the efforts of the Arya Samaj to bring back to the Hindu fold (*shuddhi*) those who had recently converted to Islam. Hindus were

The Lucknow Pact

The Lucknow Pact of December 1916 was an understanding between the Congress and the Muslim League (controlled by the UP-based "Young Party") whereby the Congress accepted separate electorates. The pact provided a joint political platform for the Moderates, Extremists and the Muslim League.

Arya Samaj

A North Indian Hindu reform organisation of the late nineteenth and early twentieth centuries, particularly active in the Punjab, which sought to revive Vedic learning and combine it with modern education in the sciences.

Music-before-mosque : The playing of music by a religious procession outside a mosque at the time of *namaz* could lead to Hindu-Muslim violence. Orthodox Muslims saw this as an interference in their peaceful communion with God.

angered by the rapid spread of *tabligh* (propaganda) and *tanzim* (organisation) after 1923. As middle class publicists and communal activists sought to build greater solidarity within their communities, mobilising people against the other community, riots spread in different parts of the country. Every communal riot deepened differences between communities, creating disturbing memories of violence.

Yet it would be incorrect to see Partition as the outcome of a simple unfolding of communal tensions. As the protagonist of *Garm Hawa*, a film on Partition, puts it, "Communal discord happened even before 1947 but it had never led to the uprooting of millions from their homes". Partition was a qualitatively different phenomenon from earlier communal politics, and to understand it we need to look carefully at the events of the last decade of British rule.

What is communalism?

There are many aspects to our identity. You are a girl or a boy, all of you are young persons, you belong to a certain village, city, district or state and speak certain languages. You are Indians but you are also world citizens. Income levels differ from family to family, hence all of us belong to some social class or the other. Most of us have a religion, and caste may play an important role in our lives. In other words, our identities have numerous features, they are complex. There are times, however, when people attach greater significance to certain chosen aspects of their identity such as religion. This in itself cannot be described as communal.

Communalism refers to a politics that seeks to unify one community around a religious identity in hostile opposition to another community. It seeks to define this community identity as fundamental and fixed. It attempts to consolidate this identity and present it as natural – as if people were born into the identity, as if the identities do not evolve through history over time. In order to unify the community, communalism suppresses distinctions within the community and emphasises the essential unity of the community against other communities.

One could say communalism nurtures a politics of hatred for an identified "other"– "Hindus" in the case of Muslim communalism, and "Muslims" in the case of Hindu communalism. This hatred feeds a politics of violence.

Communalism, then, is a particular kind of politicisation of religious identity, an ideology that seeks to promote conflict between religious communities. In the context of a multi-religious country, the phrase "religious nationalism" can come to acquire a similar meaning. In such a country, any attempt to see a religious community as a nation would mean sowing the seeds of antagonism against some other religion/s.

3.2 The provincial elections of 1937 and the Congress ministries

In 1937, elections to the provincial legislatures were held for the first time. Only about 10 to 12 per cent of the population enjoyed the right to vote. The Congress did well in the elections, winning an absolute majority in five out of eleven provinces and forming governments in seven of them. It did badly in the constituencies reserved for Muslims, but the Muslim League also fared poorly, polling only 4.4 per cent of the total Muslim vote cast in this election. The League failed to win a single seat in the North West Frontier Province (NWFP) and could capture only two out of 84 reserved constituencies in the Punjab and three out of 33 in Sind.

In the United Provinces, the Muslim League wanted to form a joint government with the Congress. The Congress had won an absolute majority in the province, so it rejected the offer. Some scholars argue that this rejection convinced the League that if India remained united, then Muslims would find it difficult to gain political power because they would remain a minority. The League assumed, of course, that only a Muslim party could represent Muslim interests, and that the Congress was essentially a Hindu party. But Jinnah's insistence that the League be recognised as the "sole spokesman" of Muslims could convince few at the time. Though popular in the United Provinces, Bombay and Madras, social support for the League was still fairly weak in three of the provinces from which Pakistan was to be carved out just ten years later – Bengal, the NWFP and the Punjab. Even in Sind it failed to form a government. It was from this point onwards that the League doubled its efforts at expanding its social support.

The Congress ministries also contributed to the widening rift. In the United Provinces, the party had rejected the Muslim League proposal for a coalition government partly because the League tended to support landlordism, which the Congress wished to abolish, although the party had not yet taken any concrete steps in that direction. Nor did the Congress achieve any substantial gains in the "Muslim mass contact" programme it launched. In the end, the secular and radical rhetoric of the Congress merely alarmed conservative Muslims and the Muslim landed elite, without winning over the Muslim masses.

The Muslim League

Initially floated in Dhaka in 1906, the Muslim League was quickly taken over by the U.P.-based Muslim elite. The party began to make demands for autonomy for the Muslim-majority areas of the subcontinent and/or Pakistan in the 1940s.

Hindu Mahasabha

Founded in 1915, the Hindu Mahasabha was a Hindu party that remained confined to North India. It aimed to unite Hindu society by encouraging the Hindus to transcend the divisions of caste and sect. It sought to define Hindu identity in opposition to Muslim identity.

Moreover, while the leading Congress leaders in the late 1930s insisted more than ever before on the need for secularism, these ideas were by no means universally shared lower down in the party hierarchy, or even by all Congress ministers. Maulana Azad, an important Congress leader, pointed out in 1937 that members of the Congress were not allowed to join the League, yet Congressmen were active in the Hindu Mahasabha– at least in the Central Provinces (present-day Madhya Pradesh). Only in December 1938 did the Congress Working Committee declare that Congress members could not be members of the Mahasabha. Incidentally, this was also the period when the Hindu Mahasabha and the Rashtriya Swayamsevak Sangh (RSS) were gaining strength. The latter spread from its Nagpur base to the United Provinces, the Punjab, and other parts of the country in the 1930s. By 1940, the RSS had over 100,000 trained and highly disciplined cadres pledged to an ideology of Hindu nationalism, convinced that India was a land of the Hindus.

3.3 The "Pakistan" Resolution

The Pakistan demand was formalised gradually. On 23 March 1940, the League moved a resolution demanding a measure of autonomy for the Muslim-majority areas of the subcontinent. This ambiguous resolution never mentioned partition or Pakistan. In fact Sikandar Hayat Khan, Punjab Premier and leader of the Unionist Party, who had drafted the resolution, declared in a Punjab assembly speech on 1 March 1941 that he was opposed to a Pakistan that would mean "Muslim Raj here and Hindu Raj elsewhere ... If Pakistan means unalloyed Muslim Raj in the Punjab then I will have nothing to do with it." He reiterated his plea for a loose (united), confederation with considerable autonomy for the confederating units.

The origins of the Pakistan demand have also been traced back to the Urdu poet Mohammad Iqbal, the writer of "*Sare Jahan Se Achha Hindustan Hamara*". In his presidential address to the Muslim League in 1930, the poet spoke of a need for a "North-West Indian Muslim state". Iqbal, however, was not visualising the emergence of a new country in that speech but a reorganisation of Muslim-majority

---

Confederation – in modern political language it refers to a union of fairly autonomous and sovereign states with a central government with delimited powers

---

The name "Pakistan"

The name Pakistan or **Pak-stan** (from **P**unjab, **A**fghan, **K**ashmir, **S**ind and Baluchi**stan**) was coined by a Punjabi Muslim student at Cambridge, Choudhry Rehmat Ali, who, in pamphlets written in 1933 and 1935, desired a separate national status for this new entity. No one took Rehmat Ali seriously in the 1930s, least of all the League and other Muslim leaders who dismissed his idea merely as a student's dream.

areas in north-western India into an autonomous unit within a single, loosely structured Indian federation.

3.4 The suddenness of Partition

We have seen that the League itself was vague about its demand in 1940. There was a very short time – just seven years – between the first formal articulation of the demand for a measure of autonomy for the Muslim-majority areas of the subcontinent and Partition. No one knew what the creation of Pakistan meant, and how it might shape people's lives in the future. Many who migrated from their homelands in 1947 thought they would return as soon as peace prevailed again.

Initially even Muslim leaders did not seriously raise the demand for Pakistan as a sovereign state. In the beginning Jinnah himself may have seen the Pakistan idea as a bargaining counter, useful for blocking possible British concessions to the Congress and gaining additional favours for the Muslims. The pressure of the Second World War on the British delayed negotiations for independence for some time. Nonetheless, it was the massive Quit India Movement which started in 1942, and persisted despite intense repression, that brought the British Raj to its knees and compelled its officials to open a dialogue with Indian parties regarding a possible transfer of power.

3.5 Post-War developments

When negotiations were begun again in 1945, the British agreed to create an entirely Indian central Executive Council, except for the Viceroy and the Commander-in-Chief of the armed forces, as a preliminary step towards full independence. Discussions about the transfer of power broke down due to Jinnah's unrelenting demand that the League had an absolute right to choose all the Muslim members of the Executive Council and that there should be a kind of communal veto in the Council, with decisions opposed by Muslims needing a two-thirds majority. Given the existing political situation, the League's first demand was quite extraordinary, for a large section of the nationalist Muslims supported the Congress (its delegation for these discussions was headed by Maulana Azad), and in West Punjab members of the Unionist Party were

Source 4

The Muslim League resolution of 1940

The League's resolution of 1940 demanded:

that geographically contiguous units are demarcated into regions, which should be so constituted, with such territorial readjustments as may be necessary, that the areas in which the Muslims are numerically in a majority as in the north-western and eastern zones of India should be grouped to constitute "Independent States", in which the constituent units shall be autonomous and sovereign.

➲ What was the League demanding? Was it demanding Pakistan as we know it today?

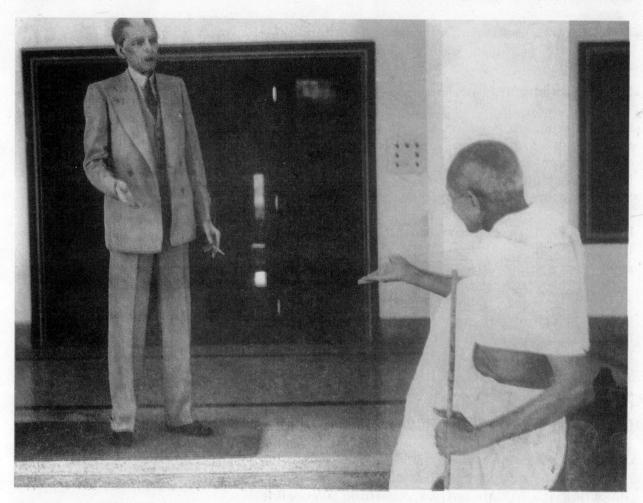

Fig. 14.6
*Mahatma Gandhi with Mohammad
Ali Jinnah before a meeting with the
Viceroy in November 1939*

largely Muslims. The British had no intention of
annoying the Unionists who still controlled the
Punjab government and had been consistently loyal
to the British.

Provincial elections were again held in 1946. The
Congress swept the general constituencies, capturing
91.3 per cent of the non-Muslim vote. The League's
success in the seats reserved for Muslims was equally
spectacular: it won all 30 reserved constituencies in
the Centre with 86.6 per cent of the Muslim vote and
442 out of 509 seats in the provinces. Only as late as
1946, therefore, did the League establish itself as the
dominant party among Muslim voters, seeking to
vindicate its claim to be the "sole spokesman" of
India's Muslims. You will, however, recall that the
franchise was extremely limited. About 10 to 12 per
cent of the population enjoyed the right to vote in the
provincial elections and a mere one per cent in the
elections for the Central Assembly.

Unionist Party

A political party representing
the interests of landholders –
Hindu, Muslim and Sikh – in
the Punjab. The party was
particularly powerful during
the period 1923-47.

3.6 A possible alternative to Partition

In March 1946 the British Cabinet sent a three-member mission to Delhi to examine the League's demand and to suggest a suitable political framework for a free India. The Cabinet Mission toured the country for three months and recommended a loose three-tier confederation. India was to remain united. It was to have a weak central government controlling only foreign affairs, defence and communications with the existing provincial assemblies being grouped into three sections while electing the constituent assembly: Section A for the Hindu-majority provinces, and Sections B and C for the Muslim-majority provinces of the north-west and the north-east (including Assam) respectively. The sections or groups of provinces would comprise various regional units. They would have the power to set up intermediate-level executives and legislatures of their own.

Initially all the major parties accepted this plan. But the agreement was short-lived because it was based on mutually opposed interpretations of the plan. The League wanted the grouping to be compulsory, with Sections B and C developing into strong entities with the right to secede from the Union in the future. The Congress wanted that provinces be given the right to join a group. It was not satisfied with the Mission's clarification that grouping would be compulsory at first, but provinces would have the right to opt out after the constitution had been finalised and new elections held in accordance with it. Ultimately, therefore, neither the League nor the Congress agreed to the Cabinet Mission's proposal. This was a most crucial juncture, because *after* this partition became more or less inevitable, with most of the Congress leaders agreeing to it, seeing it as tragic but unavoidable. Only Mahatma Gandhi and Khan Abdul Ghaffar Khan of the NWFP continued to firmly oppose the idea of partition.

Secede means to withdraw formally from an association or organisation.

Fig. 14.7
Mahatma Gandhi in the NWFP, October 1938 with Khan Abdul Ghaffar Khan (who came to be known as Frontier Gandhi), Sushila Nayar and Amtus Salem

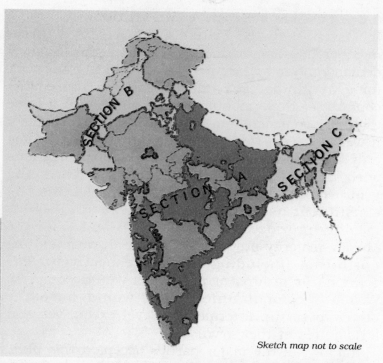

Sketch map not to scale

Map 1
The Cabinet Mission proposal for an Indian federation with three sections

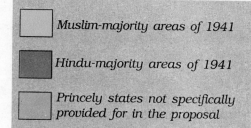

☐ *Muslim-majority areas of 1941*

☐ *Hindu-majority areas of 1941*

☐ *Princely states not specifically provided for in the proposal*

Source 5

"A voice in the wilderness"

Mahatma Gandhi knew that his was "a voice in the wilderness" but he nevertheless continued to oppose the idea of Partition:

> But what a tragic change we see today. I wish the day may come again when Hindus and Muslims will do nothing without mutual consultation. I am day and night tormented by the question what I can do to hasten the coming of that day. I appeal to the League not to regard any Indian as its enemy ... Hindus and Muslims are born of the same soil. They have the same blood, eat the same food, drink the same water and speak the same language.

SPEECH AT PRAYER MEETING, 7 SEPTEMBER 1946,
CWMG, VOL. 92, P.139

> But I am firmly convinced that the Pakistan demand as put forward by the Muslim League is un-Islamic and I have not hesitated to call it sinful. Islam stands for the unity and brotherhood of mankind, not for disrupting the oneness of the human family. Therefore, those who want to divide India into possible warring groups are enemies alike of Islam and India. They may cut me to pieces but they cannot make me subscribe to something which I consider to be wrong.

HARIJAN, 26 SEPTEMBER 1946, *CWMG*, VOL. 92, P.229

➲ What are the arguments that Mahatma Gandhi offers in opposing the idea of Pakistan?

3.7 Towards Partition

After withdrawing its support to the Cabinet Mission plan, the Muslim League decided on "Direct Action" for winning its Pakistan demand. It announced 16 August 1946 as "Direct Action Day". On this day, riots broke out in Calcutta, lasting several days and leaving several thousand people dead. By March 1947 violence spread to many parts of northern India.

It was in March 1947 that the Congress high command voted for dividing the Punjab into two halves, one with Muslim majority and the other with Hindu/Sikh majority; and it asked for the application of a similar principle to Bengal. By this time, given the numbers game, many Sikh leaders and Congressmen in the Punjab were convinced that Partition was a necessary evil, otherwise they would be swamped by Muslim majorities and Muslim leaders would dictate terms. In Bengal too a section of *bhadralok* Bengali Hindus, who wanted political power to remain with them, began to fear the "permanent tutelage of Muslims" (as one of their leaders put it). Since they were in a numerical minority, they felt that only a division of the province could ensure their political dominance.

Fig. 14.8
Rioters armed with iron rods and lathis on the streets of Calcutta, August 1946

⊃ Discuss...

It is evident from a reading of section 3 that a number of factors led to Partition. Which of these do you think were the most important and why?

4. THE WITHDRAWAL OF LAW AND ORDER

Fig. 14.9
Through those blood-soaked months of 1946, violence and arson spread, killing thousands.

"Without a shot being fired"

This is what Moon wrote:

For over twenty-four hours riotous mobs were allowed to rage through this great commercial city unchallenged and unchecked. The finest bazaars were burnt to the ground without a shot being fired to disperse the incendiaries (i.e. those who stirred up conflict). The ... District Magistrate marched his (large police) force into the city and marched it out again without making any effective use of it at all ...

The bloodbath continued for about a year from March 1947 onwards. One main reason for this was the collapse of the institutions of governance. Penderel Moon, an administrator serving in Bahawalpur (in present-day Pakistan) at the time, noted how the police failed to fire even a single shot when arson and killings were taking place in Amritsar in March 1947.

Amritsar district became the scene of bloodshed later in the year when there was a complete breakdown of authority in the city. British officials did not know how to handle the situation: they were unwilling to take decisions, and hesitant to intervene. When panic-stricken people appealed for help, British officials asked them to contact Mahatma Gandhi, Jawaharlal Nehru, Vallabh Bhai Patel or M.A. Jinnah. Nobody knew who could exercise authority and power. The top leadership of the Indian parties, barring Mahatma Gandhi, were involved in negotiations regarding independence while many Indian civil servants in the affected provinces feared for their own lives and property. The British were busy preparing to quit India.

Problems were compounded because Indian soldiers and policemen came to act as Hindus, Muslims or Sikhs. As communal tension mounted, the professional commitment of those in uniform could not be relied upon. In many places not only did policemen help their co-religionists but they also attacked members of other communities.

4.1 The one-man army

Amidst all this turmoil, one man's valiant efforts at restoring communal harmony bore fruit. The 77-year-old Gandhiji decided to stake his all in a bid to vindicate his lifelong principle of non-violence, and his conviction that people's hearts could be changed. He moved from the villages of Noakhali in East Bengal (present-day Bangladesh) to the villages of Bihar and then to the riot-torn slums of Calcutta and Delhi, in a heroic effort to stop Hindus and Muslims kill each other, careful everywhere to reassure the minority community. In October 1946, Muslims in East Bengal targeted Hindus. Gandhiji visited the area, toured the villages on foot, and persuaded the local Muslims to guarantee the safety of Hindus. Similarly, in other places such as Delhi he tried to build a spirit of mutual trust and

Fig. 14.10
Villagers of Noakhali hope for a glimpse of Mahatma Gandhi

*Fig. 14.11
Villagers of a riot-torn village
awaiting the arrival of Mahatma
Gandhi*

➲ Discuss...
What did the British do to
maintain peace when they
were quitting India? And
what did Mahatma Gandhi do
in those trying times?

confidence between the two
communities. A Delhi Muslim,
Shahid Ahmad Dehlavi, compelled
to flee to a dirty, overcrowded
camp in Purana Qila, likened
Gandhiji's arrival in Delhi on
9 September 1947 to "the arrival
of the rains after a particularly
long and harsh summer". Dehlavi
recalled in his memoir how
Muslims said to one another:
"Delhi will now be saved".

On 28 November 1947, on
the occasion of Guru Nanak's
birthday, when Gandhiji went to
address a meeting of Sikhs at
Gurdwara Sisganj, he noticed that there was no
Muslim on the Chandni Chowk road, the heart of
old Delhi. "What could be more shameful for us,"
he asked during a speech that evening, "than the
fact that not a single Muslim could be found in
Chandni Chowk?" Gandhiji continued to be in Delhi,
fighting the mentality of those who wished to drive
out every Muslim from the city, seeing them as
Pakistani. When he began a fast to bring about a
change of heart, amazingly, many Hindu and Sikh
migrants fasted with him.

The effect of the fast was "electric", wrote Maulana
Azad. People began realising the folly of the pogrom
they had unleashed on the city's Muslims but it was
only Gandhiji's martyrdom that finally ended this
macabre drama of violence. "The world veritably
changed," many Delhi Muslims of the time recalled later.

5. GENDERING PARTITION

5.1 "Recovering" women
In the last decade and a half, historians have been
examining the experiences of ordinary people during
the Partition. Scholars have written about the
harrowing experiences of women in those violent
times. Women were raped, abducted, sold, often many
times over, forced to settle down to a new life
with strangers in unknown circumstances. Deeply
traumatised by all that they had undergone, some
began to develop new family bonds in their changed

circumstances. But the Indian and Pakistani governments were insensitive to the complexities of human relationships. Believing the women to be on the wrong side of the border, they now tore them away from their new relatives, and sent them back to their earlier families or locations. They did not consult the concerned women, undermining their right to take decisions regarding their own lives. According to one estimate, 30,000 women were "recovered" overall, 22,000 Muslim women in India and 8000 Hindu and Sikh women in Pakistan, in an operation that ended as late as 1954.

Source 7

Fig. 14.12
Women console each other as they hear of the death of their family members.
Males died in larger numbers in the violence of rioting.

What "recovering" women meant

Here is the experience of a couple, recounted by Prakash Tandon in his *Punjabi Century*, an autobiographical social history of colonial Punjab:

In one instance, a Sikh youth who had run amuck during the Partition persuaded a massacring crowd to let him take away a young, beautiful Muslim girl. They got married, and slowly fell in love with each other. Gradually memories of her parents, who had been killed, and her former life faded. They were happy together, and a little boy was born. Soon, however, social workers and the police, labouring assiduously to recover abducted women, began to track down the couple. They made inquiries in the Sikh's home-district of Jalandhar; he got scent of it and the family ran away to Calcutta. The social workers reached Calcutta. Meanwhile, the couple's friends tried to obtain a stay-order from the court but the law was taking its ponderous course. From Calcutta the couple escaped to some obscure Punjab village, hoping that the police would fail to shadow them. But the police caught up with them and began to question them. His wife was expecting again and now nearing her time. The Sikh sent the little boy to his mother and took his wife to a sugar-cane field. He made her as comfortable as he could in a pit while he lay with a gun, waiting for the police, determined not to lose her while he was alive. In the pit he delivered her with his own hands. The next day she ran high fever, and in three days she was dead. He had not dared to take her to the hospital. He was so afraid the social workers and the police would take her away.

5.2 Preserving "honour"

Scholars have also shown how ideas of preserving community honour came into play in this period of extreme physical and psychological danger. This notion of honour drew upon a conception of masculinity defined as ownership of *zan* (women) and *zamin* (land), a notion of considerable antiquity in North Indian peasant societies. Virility, it was believed, lay in the ability to protect your possessions – *zan* and *zamin* – from being appropriated by outsiders. And quite frequently, conflict ensued over these two prime "possessions". Often enough, women internalised the same values.

At times, therefore, when the men feared that "their" women – wives, daughters, sisters – would be violated by the "enemy", they killed the women themselves. Urvashi Butalia in her book, *The Other Side of Silence*, narrates one such gruesome incident in the village of Thoa Khalsa, Rawalpindi district. During Partition, in this Sikh village, ninety women are said to have "voluntarily" jumped into a well rather than fall into "enemy" hands. The migrant refugees from this village still commemorate the event at a gurdwara in Delhi, referring to the deaths as martyrdom, not suicide. They believe that men at that time had to courageously accept the decision of women, and in some cases even persuade the women to kill themselves. On 13 March every year, when their "martyrdom" is celebrated, the incident is recounted to an audience of men, women and children. Women are exhorted to remember the sacrifice and bravery of their sisters and to cast themselves in the same mould.

For the community of survivors, the remembrance ritual helps keep the memory alive. What such rituals do not seek to remember, however, are the stories of all those who did not wish to die, and had to end their lives against their will.

➲ Discuss...

What ideas led to the death and suffering of so many innocent women during the Partition?
Why did the Indian and Pakistani governments agree to exchange "their" women?
Do you think they were right in doing so?

6. REGIONAL VARIATIONS

The experiences of ordinary people we have been discussing so far relate to the north-western part of the subcontinent. What was the Partition like in Bengal, Uttar Pradesh, Bihar, Central India and the Deccan? While carnages occurred in Calcutta and Noakhali in 1946, the Partition was most bloody and destructive in the Punjab. The near-total displacement of Hindus and Sikhs eastwards into India from West Punjab and of almost all Punjabi-speaking Muslims to Pakistan happened in a relatively short period of two years between 1946 and 1948.

Many Muslim families of Uttar Pradesh, Bihar, Madhya Pradesh and Hyderabad in Andhra Pradesh continued to migrate to Pakistan through the 1950s and early 1960s, although many chose to remain in India. Most of these Urdu-speaking people, known as *muhajirs* (migrants) in Pakistan moved to the Karachi-Hyderabad region in Sind.

In Bengal the migration was even more protracted, with people moving across a porous border. This also meant that the Bengali division produced a process of suffering that may have been less concentrated but was as agonising. Furthermore, unlike the Punjab, the exchange of population in Bengal was not near-total. Many Bengali Hindus remained in East Pakistan while many Bengali Muslims continued to live in West Bengal. Finally, Bengali Muslims (East Pakistanis) rejected Jinnah's two-nation theory through political action, breaking away from Pakistan and creating Bangladesh in 1971-72. A common religion could not hold East and West Pakistan together.

There is, however, a huge similarity between the Punjab and Bengal experiences. In both these states, women and girls became prime targets of persecution. Attackers treated women's bodies as territory to be conquered. Dishonouring women of a community was seen as dishonouring the community itself, and a mode of taking revenge.

Fig. 14.13
Faces of despair
A massive refugee camp was set up in Purana Qila in 1947 as migrants came pouring in from different places.

Fiction, Poetry, Films

Are you familiar with any short stories, novels, poems or films about Partition? More often than not, Partition literature and films represent this cataclysmic event in more insightful ways than do the works of historians. They seek to understand mass suffering and pain by focusing on an individual protagonist or small groups of ordinary people whose destinies were shaped by a big event over which they seemed to have no control. They record the anguish and the ambiguities of the times, the incomprehensible choices that many were confronted with. They register a sense of shock and bewilderment at the scale and magnitude of the violence, at human debasement and depravity. They also speak of hope and of the ways in which people overcame adversity.

Saadat Hasan Manto, a particularly gifted Urdu short-story writer, has this to say about his work:

> For a long time I refused to accept the consequences of the revolution which was set off by the partition of the country. I still feel the same way; but I suppose, in the end, I came to accept this nightmarish reality without self-pity or despair. In the process I tried to retrieve from this man-made sea of blood, pearls of a rare hue, by writing about the single-minded dedication with which men had killed men, about the remorse felt by some of them, about the tears shed by murderers who could not understand why they still had some human feelings left. All this and more, I put in my book, *Siyah Hashiye* (Black Margins).

Partition literature and films exist in many languages, notably in Hindi, Urdu, Punjabi, Sindhi, Bengali, Assamese and English. You may want to read writers such as Manto, Rajinder Singh Bedi (Urdu), Intizar Husain (Urdu), Bhisham Sahni (Hindi), Kamaleshwar (Hindi), Rahi Masoom Raza (Hindi), Narain Bharati (Sindhi), Sant Singh Sikhon (Punjabi), Narendranath Mitra (Bengali), Syed Waliullah (Bengali), Lalithambika Antharjanam (Malayalam), Amitav Ghosh (English) and Bapsi Sidhwa (English). Amrita Pritam, Faiz Ahmed Faiz and Dinesh Das have written memorable poems on Partition in Punjabi, Urdu and Bengali respectively. You may also want to see films directed by Ritwik Ghatak (*Meghe Dhaka Tara* and *Subarnarekha)*, M.S. Sathyu (*Garam Hawa*), Govind Nihalani (*Tamas*), and a play, *Jis Lahore Nahin Vekhya O Jamya-e-nai* (He Who Has Not Seen Lahore, Has Not Been Born) directed by Habib Tanvir.

➲ Discuss...
Was your state or any neighbouring state affected by Partition? Find out how it affected the lives of men and women in the region and how they coped with the situation.

7. HELP, HUMANITY, HARMONY

Buried under the debris of the violence and pain of Partition is an enormous history of help, humanity and harmony. Many narratives such as Abdul Latif's poignant testimony, with which we began, reveal this. Historians have discovered numerous stories of how people helped each other during the Partition period, stories of caring and sharing, of the opening of new opportunities, and of triumph over trauma.

Consider, for instance, the work of Khushdeva Singh, a Sikh doctor specialising in the treatment of tuberculosis, posted at Dharampur in present-day Himachal Pradesh. Immersing himself in his work day and night, the doctor provided that rare healing touch, food, shelter, love and security to numerous migrants, Muslim, Sikh, Hindu alike. The residents of Dharampur developed the kind of faith and confidence in his humanity and generosity that the Delhi Muslims and others had in Gandhiji. One of them, Muhammad Umar, wrote to Khushdeva Singh: "With great humility I beg to state that I do not feel myself safe except under your protection. Therefore, in all kindness, be good enough to grant me a seat in your hospital."

We know about the gruelling relief work of this doctor from a memoir he entitled *Love is Stronger than Hate: A Remembrance of 1947*. Here, Singh describes his work as "humble efforts I made to discharge my duty as a human being to fellow human beings". He speaks most warmly of two short visits to Karachi in 1949. Old friends and those whom he

Source 8

A small basket of grapes

This is what Khushdeva Singh writes about his experience during one of his visits to Karachi in 1949:

My friends took me to a room at the airport where we all sat down and talked ... (and) had lunch together. I had to travel from Karachi to London ... at 2.30 a.m. ... At 5.00 p.m. ... I told my friends that they had given me so generously of their time, I thought it would be too much for them to wait the whole night and suggested they must spare themselves the trouble. But nobody left until it was dinner time ... Then they said they were leaving and that I must have a little rest before emplaning. ... I got up at about 1.45 a.m. and, when I opened the door, I saw that all of them were still there ... They all accompanied me to the plane, and, before parting, presented me with a small basket of grapes. I had no words to express my gratitude for the overwhelming affection with which I was treated and the happiness this stopover had given me.

Fig. 14.14
The refugee camps everywhere overflowed with people who needed not just food and shelter, but also love and compassion.

⊃ Discuss...
Find out more about ways in
which people supported one
another and saved lives
during Partition.

had helped at Dharampur spent a few memorable
hours with him at Karachi airport. Six police
constables, earlier acquaintances, walked him to the
plane, saluting him as he entered it. "I acknowledged
(the salute) with folded hands and tears in my eyes."

8. ORAL TESTIMONIES AND HISTORY

Have you taken note of the materials from which the
history of Partition has been constructed in this
chapter? Oral narratives, memoirs, diaries, family
histories, first-hand written accounts – all these help
us understand the trials and tribulations of ordinary
people during the partition of the country. Millions
of people viewed Partition in terms of the suffering
and the challenges of the times. For them, it was no
mere constitutional division or just the party politics
of the Muslim League, Congress and others. For them,
it meant the unexpected alterations in life as it
unfolded between 1946 and 1950 and beyond,
requiring psychological, emotional and social
adjustments. As with the Holocaust in Germany, we
should understand Partition not simply as a political
event, but also through the meanings attached to it
by those who lived it. Memories and experiences
shape the reality of an event.

One of the strengths of personal reminiscence –
one type of oral source – is that it helps us grasp
experiences and memories in detail. It enables
historians to write richly textured, vivid accounts
of what happened to people during events such as
Partition. It is impossible to extract this kind of
information from government documents. The
latter deal with policy and party matters and
various state-sponsored schemes. In the case of
Partition, government reports and files as well as
the personal writings of its high-level functionaries
throw ample light on negotiations between the
British and the major political parties about the
future of India or on the rehabilitation of refugees.
They tell us little, however, about the day-to-day
experiences of those affected by the government's
decision to divide the country.

Oral history also allows historians to broaden the
boundaries of their discipline by rescuing from
oblivion the lived experiences of the poor and the
powerless: those of, say, Abdul Latif's father; the
women of Thoa Khalsa; the refugee who retailed

wheat at wholesale prices, eking out a paltry living by selling the gunny bags in which the wheat came; a middle-class Bengali widow bent double over road-laying work in Bihar; a Peshawari trader who thought it was wonderful to land a petty job in Cuttack upon migrating to India but asked: "Where is Cuttack, is it on the upper side of Hindustan or the lower; we haven't quite heard of it before in Peshawar?"

Thus, moving beyond the actions of the well off and the well known, the oral history of Partition has succeeded in exploring the experiences of those men and women whose existence has hitherto been ignored, taken for granted, or mentioned only in passing in mainstream history. This is significant because the histories that we read often regard the life and work of the mass of the people in the past as inaccessible or unimportant.

Yet, many historians still remain sceptical of oral history. They dismiss it because oral data seem to lack concreteness and the chronology they yield may be imprecise. Historians argue that the uniqueness of personal experience makes generalisation difficult: a large picture cannot be built from such micro-evidence, and one witness is no witness. They also think oral accounts are concerned with tangential issues, and that the small individual experiences which remain in memory are irrelevant to the unfolding of larger processes of history.

However, with regard to events such as the Partition in India and the Holocaust in Germany, there is no dearth of testimony about the different forms of distress that numerous people faced. So, there is ample evidence to figure out trends, to point out exceptions. By comparing statements, oral or written, by corroborating what they yield with findings from other sources, and by being vigilant about internal contradictions, historians can weigh the reliability of a given piece of evidence. Furthermore, if history has to accord presence to the ordinary and powerless, then the oral history of Partition is not concerned with tangential matters. The experiences it relates are central to the story, so much so that oral sources should be used to check other sources and vice versa. Different types of sources have to be tapped for answering different types of questions. Government reports, for instance, will tell us of the number of "recovered" women exchanged by the Indian and Pakistani states but it is the women who will tell us about their suffering.

We must realise, however, that oral data on Partition are not automatically or easily available. They have to be obtained through interviews that need to combine empathy with tact. In this context, one of the first difficulties is that protagonists may not want to talk about intensely personal experiences. Why, for instance, would a woman who has been raped want to disclose her tragedy to a total stranger? Interviewers have to often avoid enquiring into personal traumas. They have to build considerable rapport with respondents before they can obtain in-depth and meaningful data. Then, there are problems of memory. What people *remember* or *forget* about an event when they are interviewed a few decades later will depend in part on their experiences of the intervening years and on what has happened to their communities and nations during those years. The oral historian faces the daunting task of having to sift the "actual" experiences of Partition from a web of "constructed" memories.

In the final analysis, many different kinds of source materials have to be used to construct a comprehensive account of Partition, so that we see it not only as an event and process, but also understand the experiences of those who lived through those traumatic times.

Fig. 14.15
Not everyone could travel by cart, not everyone could walk...

TIMELINE

1930	The Urdu poet Mohammad Iqbal speaks of the need for a "North-West Indian Muslim state" as an autonomous unit within a single, loose Indian federation
1933	The name Pakistan or *Pak-stan* is coined by a Punjabi Muslim student at Cambridge, Choudhry Rehmat Ali
1937-39	Congress ministries come to power in seven out of 11 provinces of British India
1940	The Muslim League moves a resolution at Lahore demanding a measure of autonomy for the Muslim-majority areas
1946	Elections are held in the provinces. The Congress wins massively in the general constituencies. The League's success in the Muslim seats is equally spectacular
March to June	The British Cabinet sends a three-member Cabinet Mission to Delhi
August	The Muslim League decides on "Direct Action" for winning Pakistan
16 August	Violence breaks out between Hindus-Sikhs and Muslims in Calcutta, lasting several days and leaving several thousand people dead
March 1947	The Congress high command votes for dividing the Punjab into Muslim-majority and Hindu/Sikh-majority halves and asks for the application of a similar principle to Bengal; the British begin to quit India
14-15 August 1947	Pakistan is formed; India gains independence. Mahatma Gandhi tours Noakhali in East Bengal to restore communal harmony

ANSWER IN 100-150 WORDS

1. What did the Muslim League demand through its resolution of 1940?

2. Why did some people think of Partition as a very sudden development?

3. How did ordinary people view Partition?

4. What were Mahatma Gandhi's arguments against Partition?

5. Why is Partition viewed as an extremely significant marker in South Asian history?

If you would like to know more, read:

Jasodhara Bagchi and Subhoranjan Dasgupta (eds.). 2003. *The Trauma and the Triumph: Gender and Partition in Eastern India.* Stree, Kolkata.

Alok Bhalla (ed.). 1994. *Stories About the Partition of India, Vols. I, II, III.* Indus (Harper Collins), New Delhi.

Urvashi Butalia. 1998. *The Other Side of Silence: Voices from the Partition of India.* Viking (Penguin Books), New Delhi.

Mushirul Hasan, ed. 1996 *India's Partition.* Oxford University Press, New Delhi.

Gyanendra Pandey. 2001. *Remembering Partition: Violence, Nationalism and History in India.* Cambridge University Press, Cambridge.

Anita Inder Singh. 2006. *The Partition of India.* National Book Trust, New Delhi.

WRITE A SHORT ESSAY (250-300 WORDS) ON THE FOLLOWING:

6. Why was British India partitioned?

7. How did women experience Partition?

8. How did the Congress come to change its views on Partition?

9. Examine the strengths and limitations of oral history. How have oral-history techniques furthered our understanding of Partition?

MAP WORK

10. On an outline map of South Asia, mark out Sections A, B and C of the Cabinet Mission proposals. How is this map different from the political map of present-day South Asia?

PROJECT (CHOOSE ONE)

11. Find out about the ethnic violence that led to the partition of Yugoslavia. Compare your findings with what you have read about Partition in this chapter.

12. Find out whether there are any communities that have migrated to your city, town, village or any near-by place. (Your area may even have people who migrated to it during Partition.) Interview members of such communities and summarise your findings in a report. Ask people about the place they came from, the reasons for their migration, and their experiences. Also find out what changes the area witnessed as a result of this migration.

FRAMING THE CONSTITUTION
THE BEGINNING OF A NEW ERA

The Indian Constitution, which came into effect on 26 January 1950, has the distinction of being the longest in the world. Its length and complexity are perhaps understandable when one considers the country's size and diversity. At Independence, India was not merely large and diverse, but also deeply divided. A Constitution designed to keep the country together, and to take it forward, had necessarily to be an elaborate, carefully-worked-out, and painstakingly drafted document. For one thing, it sought to heal wounds of the past and the present, to make Indians of different classes, castes and communities come together in a shared political experiment. For another, it sought to nurture democratic institutions in what had long been a culture of hierarchy and deference.

The Constitution of India was framed between December 1946 and December 1949. During this time its drafts were discussed clause by clause in the Constituent Assembly of India. In all, the Assembly

Fig. 15.1
The Constitution was signed in December 1949 after three years of debate.

held eleven sessions, with sittings spread over 165 days. In between the sessions, the work of revising and refining the drafts was carried out by various committees and sub-committees.

From your political science textbooks you know what the Constitution of India is, and you have seen how it has worked over the decades since Independence. This chapter will introduce you to the history that lies behind the Constitution, and the intense debates that were part of its making. If we try and hear the voices within the Constituent Assembly, we get an idea of the process through which the Constitution was framed and the vision of the new nation formulated.

Fig. 15.2
Images of desolation and destruction continued to haunt members of the Constituent Assembly.

1. A TUMULTUOUS TIME

The years immediately preceding the making of the Constitution had been exceptionally tumultuous: a time of great hope, but also of abject disappointment. On 15 August 1947, India had been made free, but it had also been divided. Fresh in popular memory were the Quit India struggle of 1942 – perhaps the most widespread popular movement against the British Raj – as well as the bid by Subhas Chandra Bose to win freedom through armed struggle with foreign aid. An even more recent upsurge had also evoked much popular sympathy – this was the rising of the ratings of the Royal Indian Navy in Bombay and other cities in the spring of 1946. Through the late 1940s there were periodic, if scattered, mass protests of workers and peasants in different parts of the country.

One striking feature of these popular upsurges was the degree of Hindu-Muslim unity they manifested. In contrast, the two leading Indian political parties, the Congress and the Muslim League, had repeatedly failed to arrive at a settlement that would bring about religious reconciliation and social harmony. The Great Calcutta Killings of August 1946 began a year of almost continuous rioting across northern and eastern India (see Chapters 13 and 14). The violence culminated in the massacres that accompanied the transfer of populations when the Partition of India was announced.

On Independence Day, 15 August 1947, there was an outburst of joy and hope, unforgettable for those who lived through that time. But innumerable Muslims in India, and Hindus and Sikhs in Pakistan, were now faced with a cruel choice – the threat of

Fig. 15.3
Jawaharlal Nehru speaking in the Constituent Assembly at midnight on14 August 1947
It was on this day that Nehru gave his famous speech that began with the following lines:
"Long years ago we made a tryst with destiny, and now the time comes when we shall redeem our pledge, not wholly or in full measure, but very substantially. At the stroke of the midnight hour, when the world sleeps, India will awake to life and freedom."

sudden death or the squeezing of opportunities on the one side, and a forcible tearing away from their age-old roots on the other. Millions of refugees were on the move, Muslims into East and West Pakistan, Hindus and Sikhs into West Bengal and the eastern half of the Punjab. Many perished before they reached their destination.

Another, and scarcely less serious, problem faced by the new nation was that of the princely states. During the period of the Raj, approximately one-third of the area of the subcontinent was under the control of nawabs and maharajas who owed allegiance to the British Crown, but were otherwise left mostly free to rule – or misrule – their territory as they wished. When the British left India, the constitutional status of these princes remained ambiguous. As one contemporary observer remarked, some maharajas now began "to luxuriate in wild dreams of independent power in an India of many partitions".

This was the background in which the Constituent Assembly met. How could the debates within the Assembly remain insulated from what was happening outside?

1.1 The making of the Constituent Assembly

The members of the Constituent Assembly were not elected on the basis of universal franchise. In the winter of 1945-46 provincial elections were held in India. The Provincial Legislatures then chose the representatives to the Constituent Assembly.

The Constituent Assembly that came into being was dominated by one party: the Congress. The

Congress swept the general seats in the provincial elections, and the Muslim League captured most of the reserved Muslim seats. But the League chose to boycott the Constituent Assembly, pressing its demand for Pakistan with a separate constitution. The Socialists too were initially unwilling to join, for they believed the Constituent Assembly was a creation of the British, and therefore incapable of being truly autonomous. In effect, therefore, 82 per cent of the members of the Constituent Assembly were also members of the Congress.

The Congress however was not a party with one voice. Its members differed in their opinion on critical issues. Some members were inspired by socialism while others were defenders of landlordism. Some were close to communal parties while others were assertively secular. Through the national movement Congress members had learnt to debate their ideas in public and negotiate their differences. Within the Constituent Assembly too, Congress members did not sit quiet.

The discussions within the Constituent Assembly were also influenced by the opinions expressed by the public. As the deliberations continued, the arguments were reported in newspapers, and the proposals were publicly debated. Criticisms and

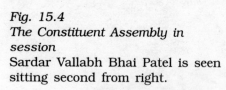

Fig. 15.4
The Constituent Assembly in session
Sardar Vallabh Bhai Patel is seen sitting second from right.

counter-criticisms in the press in turn shaped the nature of the consensus that was ultimately reached on specific issues. In order to create a sense of collective participation the public was also asked to send in their views on what needed to be done. Many of the linguistic minorities wanted the protection of their mother tongue, religious minorities asked for special safeguards, while dalits demanded an end to all caste oppression and reservation of seats in government bodies. Important issues of cultural rights and social justice raised in these public discussions were debated on the floor of the Assembly.

1.2 The dominant voices

The Constituent Assembly had 300 members. Of these, six members played particularly important roles. Three were representatives of the Congress, namely, Jawaharlal Nehru, Vallabh Bhai Patel and Rajendra Prasad. It was Nehru who moved the crucial "Objectives Resolution", as well as the resolution proposing that the National Flag of India be a "horizontal tricolour of saffron, white and dark green in equal proportion", with a wheel in navy blue at the centre. Patel, on the other hand, worked mostly behind the scenes, playing a key role in the drafting of several reports, and working to reconcile opposing points of view. Rajendra Prasad's role was as President of the Assembly, where he had to steer the discussion along constructive lines while making sure all members had a chance to speak.

Besides this Congress trio, a very important member of the Assembly was the lawyer and economist B.R. Ambedkar. During the period of British rule, Ambedkar had been a political opponent of the Congress; but, on the advice of Mahatma Gandhi, he was asked at Independence to join the Union Cabinet as law minister. In this capacity, he served as Chairman of the Drafting Committee of the Constitution. Serving with him were two other lawyers, K.M. Munshi from Gujarat and Alladi Krishnaswamy Aiyar from Madras, both of whom gave crucial inputs in the drafting of the Constitution.

These six members were given vital assistance by two civil servants. One was B. N. Rau, Constitutional Advisor to the Government of India, who prepared a series of background papers based on a close study of the political systems obtaining in other countries.

The other was the Chief Draughtsman, S. N. Mukherjee, who had the ability to put complex proposals in clear legal language.

Ambedkar himself had the responsibility of guiding the Draft Constitution through the Assembly. This took three years in all, with the printed record of the discussions taking up eleven bulky volumes. But while the process was long it was also extremely interesting. The members of the Constituent Assembly were eloquent in expressing their sometimes very divergent points of view. In their presentations we can discern many conflicting ideas of India – of what language Indians should speak, of what political and economic systems the nation should follow, of what moral values its citizens should uphold or disavow.

Fig. 15.5
B. R. Ambedkar presiding over a discussion of the Hindu Code Bill

⊃ Discuss...
Look again at Chapters 13 and 14. Discuss how the political situation of the time may have shaped the nature of the debates within the Constituent Assembly.

2. THE VISION OF THE CONSTITUTION

On 13 December 1946, Jawaharlal Nehru introduced the "Objectives Resolution" in the Constituent Assembly. It was a momentous resolution that outlined the defining ideals of the Constitution of Independent India, and provided the framework within which the work of constitution-making was to proceed. It proclaimed India to be an "Independent Sovereign Republic", guaranteed its citizens justice, equality and freedom, and assured that "adequate safeguards shall be provided for minorities, backward and tribal areas, and Depressed and Other Backward Classes ... " After outlining these objectives, Nehru placed the Indian experiment in a broad historical perspective. As he spoke, he said, his mind went back to the historic efforts in the past to produce such documents of rights.

Source 1

"We are not going just to copy"

This is what Jawaharlal Nehru said in his famous speech of 13 December 1946:

My mind goes back to the various Constituent Assemblies that have gone before and of what took place at the making of the great American nation when the fathers of that nation met and fashioned out a Constitution which has stood the test of so many years, more than a century and a half, and of the great nation which has resulted, which has been built up on the basis of that Constitution. My mind goes back to that mighty revolution which took place also over 150 years ago and to that Constituent Assembly that met in that gracious and lovely city of Paris which has fought so many battles for freedom, to the difficulties that that Constituent Assembly had and to how the King and other authorities came in its way, and still it continued. The House will remember that when these difficulties came and even the room for a meeting was denied to the then Constituent Assembly, they betook themselves to an open tennis court and met there and took the oath, which is called the Oath of the Tennis Court, that they continued meeting in spite of Kings, in spite of the others, and did not disperse till they had finished the task they had undertaken. Well, I trust that it is in that solemn spirit that we too are meeting here and that we, too, whether we meet in this chamber or other chambers, or in the fields or in the market-place, will go on meeting and continue our work till we have finished it.

contd

Source 1 (contd)

Then my mind goes back to a more recent revolution which gave rise to a new type of State, the revolution that took place in Russia and out of which has arisen the Union of the Soviet Socialist Republics, another mighty country which is playing a tremendous part in the world, not only a mighty country but for us in India, a neighbouring country.

So our mind goes back to these great examples and we seek to learn from their success and to avoid their failures. Perhaps we may not be able to avoid failures because some measure of failure is inherent in human effort. Nevertheless, we shall advance, I am certain, in spite of obstructions and difficulties, and achieve and realise the dream that we have dreamt so long ...

We say that it is our firm and solemn resolve to have an independent sovereign republic. India is bound to be sovereign, it is bound to be independent and it is bound to be a republic ... Now, some friends have raised the question: "Why have you not put in the word 'democratic' here.?" Well, I told them that it is conceivable, of course, that a republic may not be democratic but the whole of our past is witness to this fact that we stand for democratic institutions. Obviously we are aiming at democracy and nothing less than a democracy. What form of democracy, what shape it might take is another matter. The democracies of the present day, many of them in Europe and elsewhere, have played a great part in the world's progress. Yet it may be doubtful if those democracies may not have to change their shape somewhat before long if they have to remain completely democratic. We are not going just to copy, I hope, a certain democratic procedure or an institution of a so-called democratic country. We may improve upon it. In any event whatever system of government we may establish here must fit in with the temper of our people and be acceptable to them. We stand for democracy. It will be for this House to determine what shape to give to that democracy, the fullest democracy, I hope. The House will notice that in this Resolution, although we have not used the word "democratic" because we thought it is obvious that the word "republic" contains that word and we did not want to use unnecessary words and redundant words, but we have done something much more than using the word. We have given the content of democracy in this Resolution and not only the content of democracy but the content, if I may say so, of economic democracy in   is Resolution. Others might take objection to this Resolution on the ground that we have not said that it should be a Socialist State. Well, I stand for Socia.... .nd, I hope, India will stand for Socialism and that India will go towards the constitution of a Socialist State and I do believe that the whole world will have to go that way.

CONSTITUENT ASSEMBLY DEBATES (CAD), VOL.I

Oath of the Tennis Court

Nehru's speech (Source 1) merits careful scrutiny. What exactly was being stated here? What did Nehru's seemingly nostalgic return to the past reflect? What was he saying about the origin of the ideas embodied in the vision of the Constitution? In returning to the past and referring to the American and French Revolutions, Nehru was locating the history of constitution-making in India within a longer history of struggle for liberty and freedom. The momentous nature of the Indian project was emphasised by linking it to revolutionary moments in the past. But Nehru was not suggesting that those events were to provide any blueprint for the present; or that the ideas of those revolutions could be mechanically borrowed and applied in India. He did not define the specific form of democracy, and suggested that this had to be decided through deliberations. And he stressed that the ideals and provisions of the constitution introduced in India could not be just derived from elsewhere. "We are not going just to copy", he said. The system of government established in India, he declared, had to "fit in with the temper of our people and be acceptable to them". It was necessary to learn from the people of the West, from their achievements and failures, but the Western nations too had to learn from experiments elsewhere, they too had to change their own notions of democracy. The objective of the Indian Constitution would be to fuse the liberal ideas of democracy with the socialist idea of economic justice, and re-adapt and re-work all these ideas within the Indian context. Nehru's plea was for creative thinking about what was appropriate for India.

2.1 The will of the people

A Communist member, Somnath Lahiri saw the dark hand of British imperialism hanging over the deliberations of the Constituent Assembly. He thus urged the members, and Indians in general, to fully free themselves from the influences of imperial rule. In the winter of 1946-47, as the Assembly deliberated, the British were still in India. An interim administration headed by Jawaharlal Nehru was in place, but it could only operate under the directions of the Viceroy and the British Government in London. Lahiri exhorted his colleagues to realise that the Constituent Assembly was British-made and was "working the British plans as the British should like it to be worked out".

> ⟳ What explanation does Jawaharlal Nehru give for not using the term "democratic" in the Objectives Resolution in Source 1?

Fig. 15.6

Members of the Interim Government
Front row (left to right): Baldev Singh, John Mathai, C Rajagopalachari, Jawaharlal Nehru,
Liaquat Ali Khan, Vallabhbhai Patel, I.I. Chundrigar, Asaf Ali, C.H. Bhabha.
Back row (left to right): Jagjivan Ram, Ghazanfar Ali Khan, Rajendra Prasad, Abdur Nishtar

Source 2

"That is very good, Sir – bold words, noble words"

Somnath Lahiri said:

Well, Sir, I must congratulate Pandit Nehru for the fine expression he gave to the spirit of the Indian people when he said that no imposition from the British will be accepted by the Indian people. Imposition would be resented and objected to, he said, and he added that if need be we will walk the valley of struggle. That is very good, Sir – bold words, noble words.

But the point is to see when and how are you going to apply that challenge. Well, Sir, the point is that the imposition is here right now. Not only has the British Plan made any future Constitution ... dependent on a treaty satisfactory to the Britisher but it suggests that for every little difference you will have to run to the Federal Court or dance attendance there in England; or to call on the British Prime Minister Clement Attlee or someone else. Not only is it a fact that this Constituent Assembly, whatever plans we may be hatching, we are under the shadow of British guns, British Army, their economic and financial stranglehold – which means that the final power is still in the British hands and the question of power has not yet been finally decided, which means the future is not yet completely in our hands. Not only that, but the statements made by Attlee and others recently have made it clear that if need be, they will even threaten you with division entirely. This means, Sir, there is no freedom in this country. As Sardar Vallabh Bhai Patel put it some days ago, we have freedom only to fight among ourselves. That is the only freedom we have got ... Therefore, our humble suggestion is that it is not a question of getting something by working out this Plan but to declare independence here and now and call upon the Interim Government, call upon the people of India, to stop fratricidal warfare and look out against its enemy, which still has the whip hand, the British Imperialism – and go together to fight it and then resolve our claims afterwards when we will be free.

CAD, VOL.I

Nehru admitted that most nationalist leaders had wanted a different kind of Constituent Assembly. It was also true, in a sense, that the British Government had a "hand in its birth", and it had attached certain conditions within which the Assembly had to function. "But," emphasised Nehru, "you must not ignore the source from which this Assembly derives its strength." Nehru added:

> Governments do not come into being by State Papers. Governments are, in fact the expression of the will of the people. We have met here today because of the strength of the people behind us and we shall go as far as the people – not of any party or group but the people as a whole – shall wish us to go. We should, therefore, always keep in mind the passions that lie in the hearts of the masses of the Indian people and try to fulfil them.

The Constituent Assembly was expected to express the aspirations of those who had participated in the movement for independence. Democracy, equality and justice were ideals that had become intimately associated with social struggles in India since the nineteenth century. When the social reformers in the nineteenth century opposed child marriage and demanded that widows be allowed to remarry, they were pleading for social justice. When Swami Vivekananda campaigned for a reform of Hinduism, he wanted religions to become more just. When Jyotiba Phule in Maharashtra pointed to the suffering of the depressed castes, or Communists and Socialists organised workers and peasants, they were demanding economic and social justice. The national movement against a government that was seen as oppressive and illegitimate was inevitably a struggle for democracy and justice, for citizens' rights and equality.

In fact, as the demand for representation grew, the British had been forced to introduce a series of constitutional reforms. A number of Acts were passed (1909, 1919 and 1935), gradually enlarging the space for Indian participation in provincial governments. The executive was made partly responsible to the provincial legislature in 1919, and almost entirely so under the Government of India Act of 1935. When elections were held in 1937, under the 1935 Act, the Congress came to power in eight out of the 11 provinces.

➲ Why does the speaker in Source 2 think that the Constituent Assembly was under the shadow of British guns?

Fig. 15.7
Edwin Montague (left) was the author of the Montague-Chelmsford Reforms of 1919 which allowed some form of representation in provincial legislative assemblies.

➲ Discuss...
What were the ideas outlined by Jawaharlal Nehru in his speech on the Objectives Resolution?

Yet we should not see an unbroken continuity between the earlier constitutional developments and what happened in the three years from 1946. While the earlier constitutional experiments were in response to the growing demand for a representative government, the Acts (1909, 1919 and 1935) were not directly debated and formulated by Indians. They were enacted by the colonial government. The electorate that elected the provincial bodies had expanded over the years, but even in 1935 it remained limited to no more than 10 to 15 per cent of the adult population: there was no universal adult franchise. The legislatures elected under the 1935 Act operated within the framework of colonial rule, and were responsible to the Governor appointed by the British. The vision that Nehru was trying to outline on 13 December 1946 was of the Constitution of an independent, sovereign Republic of India.

3. DEFINING RIGHTS

How were the rights of individual citizens to be defined? Were the oppressed groups to have any special rights? What rights would minorities have? Who, in fact, could be defined as a minority? As the debate on the floor of the Constituent Assembly unfolded, it was clear that there were no collectively shared answers to any of these questions. The answers were evolved through the clash of opinions and the drama of individual encounters. In his inaugural speech, Nehru had invoked the "will of the people" and declared that the makers of the Constitution had to fulfil "the passions that lie in the hearts of the masses". This was no easy task. With the anticipation of Independence, different groups expressed their will in different ways, and made different demands. These would have to be debated and conflicting ideas would have to be reconciled, before a consensus could be forged.

3.1 The problem with separate electorates

On 27 August 1947, B. Pocker Bahadur from Madras made a powerful plea for continuing separate electorates. Minorities exist in all lands, argued Bahadur; they could not be wished away, they could not be "erased out of existence". The need was to create a political framework in which minorities could live in harmony with others, and the differences between communities could be minimised. This was possible only if minorites were well represented within the political system, their voices heard, and their views taken into account. Only separate electorates would ensure that Muslims had a meaningful voice in the governance of the country. The needs of Muslims, Bahadur felt, could not be properly understood by non-Muslims; nor could a true representative of Muslims be chosen by people who did not belong to that community.

This demand for separate electorates provoked anger and dismay amongst most nationalists. In the passionate debate that followed, a range of arguments were offered against the demand. Most nationalists saw separate electorates as a measure deliberately introduced by the British to divide the people. "The English played their game under the cover of safeguards," R.V. Dhulekar told Bahadur. "With the help of it they allured you (the minorities) to a long lull. Give it up now ... Now there is no one to misguide you."

Partition had made nationalists fervently opposed to the idea of separate electorates. They were haunted by the fear of continued civil war, riots and violence. Separate electorates was a "poison that has entered the body politic of our country", declared Sardar Patel. It was a demand that had turned one community against another, divided the nation, caused bloodshed, and led to the tragic partition of the country. "Do you want peace in this land? If so do away with it (separate electorates)," urged Patel.

Fig. 15.8
In the winter of 1946 Indian leaders went to London for what turned out to be a fruitless round of talks with British Prime Minister Attlee. (Left to right: Liaquat Ali, Mohammad Ali Jinnah, Baldev Singh and Pethick-Lawrence)

Source 3

"The British element is gone, but they have left the mischief behind"

Sardar Vallabh Bhai Patel said:

It is no use saying that we ask for separate electorates, because it is good for us. We have heard it long enough. We have heard it for years, and as a result of this agitation we are now a separate nation ... Can you show me one free country where there are separate electorates? If so, I shall be prepared to accept it. But in this unfortunate country if this separate electorate is going to be persisted in, even after the division of the country, woe betide the country; it is not worth living in. Therefore, I say, it is not for my good alone, it is for your own good that I say it, forget the past. One day, we may be united ... The British element is gone, but they have left the mischief behind. We do not want to perpetuate that mischief. (Hear, hear). When the British introduced this element they had not expected that they will have to go so soon. They wanted it for their easy administration. That is all right. But they have left the legacy behind. Are we to get out of it or not?

CAD, VOL.V

Countering the demand for separate electorates, Govind Ballabh Pant declared that it was not only harmful for the nation but also for the minorities. He agreed with Bahadur that the success of a democracy was to be judged by the confidence it generated amongst different sections of people. He agreed too that every citizen in a free state should be treated in a manner that satisfied "not only his material wants but also his spiritual sense of self-respect", and that the majority community had an obligation to try and understand the problems of minorities, and empathise with their aspirations. Yet Pant opposed the idea of separate electorates. It was a suicidal demand, he argued, that would permanently isolate the minorities, make them vulnerable, and deprive them of any effective say within the government.

Source 4

"I believe separate electorates will be suicidal to the minorities"

During the debate on 27 August 1947, Govind Ballabh Pant said:

I believe separate electorates will be suicidal to the minorities and will do them tremendous harm. If they are isolated for ever, they can never convert themselves into a majority and the feeling of frustration will cripple them even from the very beginning. What is it that you desire and what is our ultimate objective? Do the minorities always want to remain as minorities or do they ever expect to form an integral part of a great nation and as such to guide and control its destinies? If they do, can they ever achieve that aspiration and that ideal if they are isolated from the rest of the community? I think it would be extremely dangerous for them if they were segregated from the rest of the community and kept aloof in an air-tight compartment where they would have to rely on others even for the air they breathe … The minorities if they are returned by separate electorates can never have any effective voice.

CAD, VOL.II

➲ Read Sources 3 and 4. What are the different arguments being put forward against separate electorates?

Behind all these arguments was the concern with the making of a unified nation state. In order to build political unity and forge a nation, every individual had to be moulded into a citizen of the State, each group had to be assimilated within the nation. The Constitution would grant to citizens rights, but citizens had to offer their loyalty to the State. Communities could be recognised as cultural entities and assured cultural rights. Politically, however, members of all communities had to act as equal members of one State, or else there would be divided loyalties. "There is the unwholesome and to some extent degrading habit of thinking always in terms of communities and never in terms of citizens," said Pant. And he added: "Let us remember that it is the citizen that must count. It is the citizen that forms the base as well as the summit of the social pyramid." Even as the importance of community rights was being recognised, there was a lurking fear among many nationalists that this may lead to divided loyalties, and make it difficult to forge a strong nation and a strong State.

Not all Muslims supported the demand for separate electorates. Begam Aizaz Rasul, for instance, felt that separate electorates were self-destructive since they isolated the minorities from the majority. By 1949, most Muslim members of the Constituent Assembly were agreed that separate electorates were against the interests of the minorities. Instead Muslims needed to take an active part in the democratic process to ensure that they had a decisive voice in the political system.

3.2 "We will need much more than this Resolution"

While welcoming the Objectives Resolution, N.G. Ranga, a socialist who had been a leader of the peasant movement, urged that the term minorities be interpreted in economic terms. The real minorities for Ranga were the poor and the downtrodden. He welcomed the legal rights the Constitution was granting to each individual but pointed to its limits. In his opinion it was meaningless for the poor people in the villages to know that they now had the fundamental right to live, and to have full employment, or that they could have their meetings, their conferences, their associations and various other civil liberties. It was essential to create conditions where these constitutionally enshrined rights could be effectively enjoyed. For this they needed protection. "They need props. They need a ladder," said Ranga.

Source 5

"There cannot be any divided loyalty"

Govind Ballabh Pant argued that in order to become loyal citizens people had to stop focusing only on the community and the self:

> For the success of democracy one must train himself in the art of self-discipline. In democracies one should care less for himself and more for others. There cannot be any divided loyalty. All loyalties must exclusively be centred round the State. If in a democracy, you create rival loyalties, or you create a system in which any individual or group, instead of suppressing his extravagance, cares nought for larger or other interests, then democracy is doomed.

CAD, VOL.II

➲ How does G. B. Pant define the attributes of a loyal citizen?

Source 6

"The real minorities are the masses of this country"

Welcoming the Objectives Resolution introduced by Jawaharlal Nehru, N.G. Ranga said:

Sir, there is a lot of talk about minorities. Who are the real minorities? Not the Hindus in the so-called Pakistan provinces, not the Sikhs, not even the Muslims. No, the real minorities are the masses of this country. These people are so depressed and oppressed and suppressed till now that they are not able to take advantage of the ordinary civil rights. What is the position? You go to the tribal areas. According to law, their own traditional law, their tribal law, their lands cannot be alienated. Yet our merchants go there, and in the so-called free market they are able to snatch their lands. Thus, even though the law goes against this snatching away of their lands, still the merchants are able to turn the tribal people into veritable slaves by various kinds of bonds, and make them hereditary bond-slaves. Let us go to the ordinary villagers. There goes the money-lender with his money and he is able to get the villagers in his pocket. There is the landlord himself, the zamindar, and the *malguzar* and there are the various other people who are able to exploit these poor villagers. There is no elementary education even among these people. These are the real minorities that need protection and assurances of protection. In order to give them the necessary protection, we will need much more than this Resolution ...

CAD, VOL.II

> ↪ **How is the notion of minority defined by Ranga?**

Ranga also drew attention to the gulf that separated the broad masses of Indians and those claiming to speak on their behalf in the Constituent Assembly:

Whom are we supposed to represent? The ordinary masses of our country. And yet most of us do not belong to the masses themselves. We are of them, we wish to stand for them, but the masses themselves are not able to come up to the Constituent Assembly. It may take some time; in the meanwhile, we are here as their trustees, as their champions, and we are trying our best to speak for them.

One of the groups mentioned by Ranga, the tribals, had among its representatives to the Assembly the gifted orator Jaipal Singh. In welcoming the Objectives Resolution, Singh said:

> ... as an Adibasi, I am not expected to understand the legal intricacies of the Resolution. But my common sense tells me that every one of us should march in that road to freedom and fight together. Sir, if there is any group of Indian people that has been shabbily treated it is my people. They have been disgracefully treated, neglected for the last 6,000 years. ... The whole history of my people is one of continuous exploitation and dispossession by the non-aboriginals of India punctuated by rebellions and disorder, and yet I take Pandit Jawaharlal Nehru at his word. I take you all at your word that now we are going to start a new chapter, a new chapter of independent India where there is equality of opportunity, where no one would be neglected.

Singh spoke eloquently on the need to protect the tribes, and ensure conditions that could help them come up to the level of the general population. Tribes were not a numerical minority, he argued, but they needed protection. They had been dispossessed of the land they had settled, deprived of their forests and pastures, and forced to move in search of new homes. Perceiving them as primitive and backward, the rest of society had turned away from them, spurned them. He made a moving plea for breaking the emotional and physical distance that separated the tribals from the rest of society: "Our point is that you have got to mix with us. We are willing to mix with you ... ". Singh was not asking for separate electorates, but he felt that reservation of seats in the legislature was essential to allow tribals to represent themselves. It would be a way, he said, of compelling others to hear the voice of tribals, and come near them.

3.3 "We were suppressed for thousands of years"
How were the rights of the Depressed Castes to be defined by the Constitution? During the national movement Ambedkar had demanded separate electorates for the Depressed Castes, and Mahatma Gandhi had opposed it, arguing that this would

Source 7

"We want removal of our social disabilities"

Dakshayani Velayudhan from Madras, argued:

What we want is not all kinds of safeguards. It is the moral safeguard which gives protection to the underdogs of this country ... I refuse to believe that seventy million Harijans are to be considered as a minority ... what we want is the ... immediate removal of our social disabilities.'

CAD, VOL.I

Source 8

We have never asked for privileges

Hansa Mehta of Bombay demanded justice for women, not reserved seats, or separate electorates.

We have never asked for privileges. What we have asked for is social justice, economic justice, and political justice. We have asked for that equality which alone can be the basis of mutual respect and understanding, without which real cooperation is not possible between man and woman.

permanently segregate them from the rest of society. How could the Constituent Assembly resolve this opposition? What kinds of protection were the Depressed Castes to be provided?

Some members of the Depressed Castes emphasised that the problem of the "Untouchables" could not be resolved through protection and safeguards alone. Their disabilities were caused by the social norms and the moral values of caste society. Society had used their services and labour but kept them at a social distance, refusing to mix with them or dine with them or allow them entry into temples. "We have been suffering, but we are prepared to suffer no more," said J. Nagappa from Madras. "We have realised our responsibilities. We know how to assert ourselves."

Nagappa pointed out that numerically the Depressed Castes were not a minority: they formed between 20 and 25 per cent of the total population. Their suffering was due to their systematic marginalisation, not their numerical insignificance. They had no access to education, no share in the administration. Addressing the assembly, K.J. Khanderkar of the Central Provinces said:

We were suppressed for thousands of years. ... suppressed... to such an extent that neither our minds nor our bodies and now even our hearts work, nor are we able to march forward. This is the position.

After the Partition violence, Ambedkar too no longer argued for separate electorates. The Constituent Assembly finally recommended that untouchability be abolished, Hindu temples be thrown open to all castes, and seats in legislatures and jobs in government offices be reserved for the lowest castes. Many recognised that this could not solve all problems: social discrimination could not be erased only through constitutional legislation, there had to be a change in the attitudes within society. But the measures were welcomed by the democratic public.

➲ Discuss...
What were the different arguments that Jaipal Singh put forward in demanding protective measures for the tribals?

4. The Powers of the State

One of the topics most vigorously debated in the Constituent Assembly was the respective rights of the Central Government and the states. Among those arguing for a strong Centre was Jawaharlal Nehru. As he put it in a letter to the President of the Constituent Assembly, "Now that partition is a settled fact, ... it would be injurious to the interests of the country to provide for a weak central authority which would be incapable of ensuring peace, of coordinating vital matters of common concern and of speaking effectively for the whole country in the international sphere".

The Draft Constitution provided for three lists of subjects: Union, State, and Concurrent. The subjects in the first list were to be the preserve of the Central Government, while those in the second list were vested with the states. As for the third list, here Centre and state shared responsibility. However, many more items were placed under exclusive Union control than in other federations, and more placed on the Concurrent list too than desired by the provinces. The Union also had control of minerals and key industries. Besides, Article 356 gave the Centre the powers to take over a state administration on the recommendation of the Governor.

The Constitution also mandated for a complex system of fiscal federalism. In the case of some taxes (for instance, customs duties and Company taxes) the Centre retained all the proceeds; in other cases (such as income tax and excise duties) it shared them with the states; in still other cases (for instance, estate duties) it assigned them wholly to the states. The states, meanwhile, could levy and collect certain taxes on their own: these included land and property taxes, sales tax and the hugely profitable tax on bottled liquor.

4.1 "The centre is likely to break"

The rights of the states were most eloquently defended by K. Santhanam from Madras. A reallocation of powers was necessary, he felt, to strengthen not only the states but also the Centre. "There is almost an obsession that by adding all kinds of powers to the Centre we can make it strong." This was a misconception, said Santhanam. If the Centre was overburdened with responsibilities, it could not function effectively. By relieving it of some of its functions, and transferring them to the states, the Centre could, in fact, be made stronger.

Source 9

Who is a better patriot?

Sir A. Ramaswamy Mudaliar from Mysore said during the debate on 21 August 1947:

Let us not lay the flattering unction to our soul that we are better patriots if we propose a strong Centre and that those who advocate a more vigorous examination of these resources are people with not enough of national spirit or patriotism.

As for the states, Santhanam felt that the proposed allocation of powers would cripple them. The fiscal provisions would impoverish the provinces since most taxes, except land revenue, had been made the preserve of the Centre. Without finances how could the states undertake any project of development? "I do not want any constitution in which the Unit has to come to the Centre and say 'I cannot educate my people. I cannot give sanitation, give me a dole for the improvement of roads, of industries.' Let us rather wipe out the federal system and let us have Unitary system." Santhanam predicted a dark future if the proposed distribution of powers was adopted without further scrutiny. In a few years, he said, all the provinces would rise in "revolt against the Centre".

Many others from the provinces echoed the same fears. They fought hard for fewer items to be put on the Concurrent and Union lists. A member from Orissa warned that "the Centre is likely to break" since powers had been excessively centralised under the Constitution.

4.2 "What we want today is a strong Government"

The argument for greater power to the provinces provoked a strong reaction in the Assembly. The need for a strong centre had been underlined on numerous occasions since the Constituent Assembly had begun its sessions. Ambedkar had declared that he wanted "a strong and united Centre (hear, hear) much stronger than the Centre we had created under the Government of India Act of 1935". Reminding the members of the riots and violence that was ripping the nation apart, many members had repeatedly stated that the powers of the Centre had to be greatly strengthened to enable it to stop the communal frenzy. Reacting to the demands for giving power to the provinces, Gopalaswami Ayyangar declared that "the Centre should be made as strong as possible". One member from the United Provinces, Balakrishna Sharma, reasoned at length that only a strong centre could plan for the well-being of the country, mobilise the available economic resources, establish a proper administration, and defend the country against foreign aggression.

Before Partition the Congress had agreed to grant considerable autonomy to the provinces. This had been part of an effort to assure the Muslim League that within the provinces where the Muslim League came to power the Centre would not interfere. After Partition most nationalists changed their position because they felt that the earlier political pressures for a decentralised structure were no longer there.

There was already a unitary system in place, imposed by the colonial government. The violence of the times gave a further push to centralisation, now seen as necessary both to forestall chaos and to plan for the country's economic development. The Constitution thus showed a distinct bias towards the rights of the Union of India over those of its constituent states.

5. THE LANGUAGE OF THE NATION

How could the nation be forged when people in different regions spoke different languages, each associated with its own cultural heritage? How could people listen to each other, or connect with each other, if they did not know each other's language? Within the Constituent Assembly, the language issue was debated over many months, and often generated intense arguments.

By the 1930s, the Congress had accepted that Hindustani ought to be the national language. Mahatma Gandhi felt that everyone should speak in a language that common people could easily understand. Hindustani – a blend of Hindi and Urdu – was a popular language of a large section of the people of India, and it was a composite language enriched by the interaction of diverse cultures. Over the years it had incorporated words and terms from very many different sources, and was therefore understood by people from various regions. This multi-cultural language, Mahatma Gandhi thought, would be the ideal language of communication between diverse communities: it could unify Hindus and Muslims, and people of the north and the south.

From the end of the nineteenth century, however, Hindustani as a language had been gradually changing. As communal conflicts deepened, Hindi and Urdu also started growing apart. On the one hand, there was a move to Sanskritise Hindi, purging it of all words of Persian and Arabic origin. On the other hand, Urdu was being increasingly Persianised. As a consequence, language became associated with the politics of religious identities. Mahatma Gandhi, however, retained his faith in the composite character of Hindustani.

⊃ Discuss...
What different arguments were put forward by those advocating a strong Centre?

Source 10

What should the qualities of a national language be ?

A few months before his death Mahatma Gandhi reiterated his views on the language question:

This Hindustani should be neither Sanskritised Hindi nor Persianised Urdu but a happy combination of both. It should also freely admit words wherever necessary from the different regional languages and also assimilate words from foreign languages, provided that they can mix well and easily with our national language. Thus our national language must develop into a rich and powerful instrument capable of expressing the whole gamut of human thought and feelings. To confine oneself to Hindi or Urdu would be a crime against intelligence and the spirit of patriotism.

HARIJANSEVAK, 12 OCTOBER 1947

5.1 A plea for Hindi

In one of the earliest sessions of the Constituent Assembly, R. V. Dhulekar, a Congressman from the United Provinces, made a strong plea that Hindi be used as the language of constitution-making. When told that not everyone in the Assembly knew the language, Dhulekar retorted: "People who are present in this House to fashion a constitution for India and do not know Hindustani are not worthy to be members of this Assembly. They better leave." As the House broke up in commotion over these remarks, Dhulekar proceeded with his speech in Hindi. On this occasion peace in the House was restored through Jawaharlal Nehru's intervention, but the language issue continued to disrupt proceedings and agitate members over the subsequent three years.

Almost three years later, on 12 September 1947, Dhulekar's speech on the language of the nation once again sparked off a huge storm. By now the Language Committee of the Constituent Assembly had produced its report and had thought of a compromise formula to resolve the deadlock between those who advocated Hindi as the national language and those who opposed it. It had decided, but not yet formally declared, that Hindi in the Devanagari script would be the official language, but the transition to Hindi would be gradual. For the first fifteen years, English would continue to be used for all official purposes. Each province was to be allowed to choose one of the regional languages for official work within the province. By referring to Hindi as the official rather that the national language, the Language Committee of the Constituent Assembly hoped to placate ruffled emotions and arrive at a solution that would be acceptable to all.

Dhulekar was not one who liked such an attitude of reconciliation. He wanted Hindi to be declared not an Official Language, but a National Language. He attacked those who protested that Hindi was being forced on the nation, and mocked at those who said, in the name of Mahatma Gandhi, that Hindustani rather than Hindi ought to be the national language.

> Sir, nobody can be more happy than myself that Hindi has become the official language of the country … Some say that it is a concession to Hindi language. I say "no". It is a consummation of a historic process.

What particularly perturbed many members was the tone in which Dhulekar was arguing his case. Several times during his speech, the President of the Assembly interrupted Dhulekar and told him: "I do not think you are advancing your case by speaking like this." But Dhulekar continued nonetheless.

5.2 The fear of domination

A day after Dhulekar spoke, Shrimati G. Durgabai from Madras explained her worries about the way the discussion was developing:

> Mr President, the question of national language for India which was an almost agreed proposition until recently has suddenly become a highly controversial issue. Whether rightly or wrongly, the people of non-Hindi-speaking areas have been made to feel that this fight, or this attitude on behalf of the Hindi-speaking areas, is a fight for effectively preventing the natural influence of other powerful languages of India on the composite culture of this nation.

Durgabai informed the House that the opposition in the south against Hindi was very strong: "The opponents feel perhaps justly that this propaganda for Hindi cuts at the very root of the provincial languages ..." Yet, she along with many others had obeyed the call of Mahatma Gandhi and carried on Hindi propaganda in the south, braved resistance, started schools and conducted classes in Hindi. "Now what is the result of it all?" asked Durgabai. "I am shocked to see this agitation against the enthusiasm with which we took to Hindi in the early years of the century." She had accepted Hindustani as the language of the people, but now that language was being changed, words from Urdu and other regional languages were being taken out. Any move that eroded the inclusive and composite character of Hindustani, she felt, was bound to create anxieties and fears amongst different language groups.

As the discussion became acrimonious, many members appealed for a spirit of accommodation. A member from Bombay, Shri Shankarrao Deo stated that as a Congressman and a follower of Mahatma Gandhi he had accepted Hindustani as a language of the nation, but he warned: "if you want my whole-hearted support (for Hindi) you must not do now anything which may raise my suspicions and which will strengthen my fears." T. A. Ramalingam Chettiar from Madras emphasised that whatever was done had to be done with caution; the cause of Hindi would not be helped if it was pushed too aggressively. The fears of the people, even if they were unjustified, had to be allayed, or else "there will be bitter feelings left behind". "When we want to live together and form a united nation," he said, "there should be mutual adjustment and no question of forcing things on people ..."

The Constitution of India thus emerged through a process of intense debate and discussion. Many of its provisions were arrived at through a process of give-and-take, by forging a middle ground between two opposed positions.

However, on one central feature of the Constitution there was substantial agreement. This was on the granting of the vote to every adult Indian. This was an unprecedented act of faith, for in other democracies the vote had been granted slowly, and in stages. In countries such as the United States and the United Kingdom, only men of property were first granted the vote; then, men with education were also allowed into the charmed circle. After a long and bitter struggle, men of working-class or peasant background were also given the right to vote. An even longer struggle was required to grant this right to women.

A second important feature of the Constitution was its emphasis on secularism. There was no ringing pronouncement of secularism in the Preamble, but operationally, its key features as understood in Indian contexts were spelled out in an exemplary manner. This was done through the carefully drafted series of Fundamental Rights to "freedom of religion" (Articles 25-28), "cultural and educational rights" (Articles 29, 30), and "rights to equality" (Articles 14, 16, 17). All religions were guaranteed equal treatment by the State and given the right to maintain charitable institutions. The State also sought to distance itself from religious communities, banning compulsory religious instructions in State-run schools and colleges, and declaring religious discrimination in employment to be illegal. However, a certain legal space was created for social reform within communities, a space that was used to ban untouchability and introduce changes in personal and family laws. In the Indian variant of political secularism, then, there has been no absolute separation of State from religion, but a kind of judicious distance between the two.

The Constituent Assembly debates help us understand the many conflicting voices that had to be negotiated in framing the Constitution, and the many demands that were articulated. They tell us about the ideals that were invoked and the principles that the makers of the Constitution operated with. But in reading these debates we need to be aware that the ideals invoked were very often re-worked according to what seemed appropriate within a context. At times the members of the Assembly also changed their ideas as the debate unfolded over three years. Hearing others argue, some members rethought their positions, opening their minds to contrary views, while others changed their views in reaction to the events around.

Fig. 15. 9
B. R. Ambedkar and Rajendra Prasad greeting each other at the time of the handing over of the Constitution

TIMELINE

1945

| 26 July | Labour Government comes into power in Britain |
| December-January | General Elections in India |

1946

16 May	Cabinet Mission announces its constitutional scheme
16 June	Cabinet Mission presents scheme for the formation of an Interim Government at the Centre
2 September	Congress forms Interim Government with Nehru as the Vice-President
13 October	Muslim League decides to join the Interim Government
3-6 December	British Prime Minister, Attlee, meets some Indian leaders; talks fail
9 December	Constituent Assembly begins its sessions

1947

29 January	Muslim League demands dissolution of Constituent Assembly
16 July	Last meeting of the Interim Government
11 August	Jinnah elected President of the Constituent Assembly of Pakistan
14 August	Pakistan Independence; celebrations in Karachi
14-15 August	At midnight India celebrates Independence

1949

| December | Constitution is signed |

 ANSWER IN 100-150 WORDS

1. What were the ideals expressed in the Objectives Resolution?

2. How was the term minority defined by different groups?

3. What were the arguments in favour of greater power to the provinces?

4. Why did Mahatma Gandhi think Hindustani should be the national language?

If you would like to know more, read:

Granville Austin. 1972. *The Indian Constitution: The Cornerstone of a Nation.* Oxford University Press, New Delhi.

5. What historical forces shaped the vision of the Constitution?

6. Discuss the different arguments made in favour of protection of the oppressed groups.

7. What connection did some of the members of the Constituent Assembly make between the political situation of the time and the need for a strong Centre?

Rajeev Bhargava. 2000. "Democratic Vision of a New Republic"in F. R. Frankel et al. eds, *Transforming India: Social and Political Dynamics of Democracy.* Oxford University Press, New Delhi.

8. How did the Constituent Assembly seek to resolve the language controversy?

Sumit Sarkar. 1983. "Indian Democracy: The Historical Inheritance" in Atul Kohli ed., *The Success of India's Democracy.* Cambridge University Press, Cambridge.

9. On a present-day political map of India, indicate the different languages spoken in each state and mark out the one that is designated as the language for official communication. Compare the present map with a map of the early 1950s. What differences do you notice? Do the differences say something about the relationship between language and the organisation of the states?

Sumit Sarkar. 1983. *Modern India: 1885-1947.* Macmillan, New Delhi.

10. Choose any one important constitutional change that has happened in recent years. Find out why the change was made, what different arguments were put forward for the change, and the historical background to the change. If you can, try and look at the Constitutional Assembly Debates (http:// parliamentofindia.nic.in/ls/debates/ debates.htm) to see how the issue was discussed at that time. Write about your findings.

11. Compare the Constitution of America, France or South Africa with the Indian Constitution, focusing on any two of the following themes: secularism, minority rights, relations between the Centre and the states. Find out how these differences and similarities are linked to the histories of the regions.

You could visit:
parliamentofindia.nic.in/ls/ debates/debates.htm

(for a digitalised version of the Constituent Assembly Debates)

CREDITS FOR ILLUSTRATIONS

Institutions
Alkazi Foundation for the Arts, New Delhi
 (Figs. 11.6; 11.8; 12.12; 12.13)
Collection Jyotindra and Juta Jain, CIVIC Archives,
 New Delhi (Fig. 13.15)
Photo Division, Government of India, New Delhi
 (Figs. 14.3; 14.10; 15.3; 15.4; 15.5; 15.9)
Nehru Memorial Museum and Library, New Delhi
 (Fig. 15.6)
The Osian's Archive and Library Collection, Mumbai
 (Figs. 11.9; 11.18; 13.17)
Victoria Memorial Museum and Library, Kolkata
 (Figs. 10.6, 10.7)

Journals
Builder (Fig. 12.26)
Punch (Figs. 11.13; 11.14; 11.17)
The Illustrated London News (Figs. 10.1; 10.10;
 10.11; 10.12; 10.13; 10.14; 10.16; 10.17; 10.18;
 10.19; 11.15; 11.16)

Books
Bayly, C.A., *The Raj: India and the British 1600-1947*
 (Figs. 10.4; 11.10; 11.11; 12.27)
Dalrymple, William, *The Last Mughal* (Fig. 11.1)
Daniell, Thomas and William, *Views of Calcutta*
 (Figs. 12.7; 12.8; 12.9; 12.19)
Evenson, Norma, *The Indian Metropolis: A View
 Toward the West* (Figs. 12.14; 12.16; 12.20;
 12.22; 12.22; 12 23; 12.25; 12.29; 12.30)
Metcalf, T.R., *An Imperial Vision: Indian Architecture
 and British Raj* (Fig. 12.28)
Publications Division, *Mahatma Gandhi* (many of
 the Figs. in Ch.14)
Ruhe, Peter, *Gandhi* (Figs. 13.7; 13.11; 13.12)
Singh, Khushwant, *Train to Pakistan* (Figs. 15.1;
 15.4; 15.12; 15.13; 15.15)